AF679082

LAW, CRIME AND LAW ENFORCEMENT

NATIONWIDE SUSPICIOUS ACTIVITY REPORTING INITIATIVE

LAW, CRIME AND LAW ENFORCEMENT

Additional books in this series can be found on Nova's website under the Series tab.

Additional E-books in this series can be found on Nova's website under the E-book tab.

INTELLIGENCE AND COUNTERINTELLIGENCE STUDIES

Additional books in this series can be found on Nova's website under the Series tab.

Additional E-books in this series can be found on Nova's website under the E-book tab.

LAW, CRIME AND LAW ENFORCEMENT

NATIONWIDE SUSPICIOUS ACTIVITY REPORTING INITIATIVE

LAURITS HARTMANN
EDITOR

nova publishers
New York

Copyright © 2013 by Nova Science Publishers, Inc.

All rights reserved. No part of this book may be reproduced, stored in a retrieval system or transmitted in any form or by any means: electronic, electrostatic, magnetic, tape, mechanical photocopying, recording or otherwise without the written permission of the Publisher.

For permission to use material from this book please contact us:
Telephone 631-231-7269; Fax 631-231-8175
Web Site: http://www.novapublishers.com

NOTICE TO THE READER

The Publisher has taken reasonable care in the preparation of this book, but makes no expressed or implied warranty of any kind and assumes no responsibility for any errors or omissions. No liability is assumed for incidental or consequential damages in connection with or arising out of information contained in this book. The Publisher shall not be liable for any special, consequential, or exemplary damages resulting, in whole or in part, from the readers' use of, or reliance upon, this material. Any parts of this book based on government reports are so indicated and copyright is claimed for those parts to the extent applicable to compilations of such works.

Independent verification should be sought for any data, advice or recommendations contained in this book. In addition, no responsibility is assumed by the publisher for any injury and/or damage to persons or property arising from any methods, products, instructions, ideas or otherwise contained in this publication.

This publication is designed to provide accurate and authoritative information with regard to the subject matter covered herein. It is sold with the clear understanding that the Publisher is not engaged in rendering legal or any other professional services. If legal or any other expert assistance is required, the services of a competent person should be sought. FROM A DECLARATION OF PARTICIPANTS JOINTLY ADOPTED BY A COMMITTEE OF THE AMERICAN BAR ASSOCIATION AND A COMMITTEE OF PUBLISHERS.

Additional color graphics may be available in the e-book version of this book.

Library of Congress Cataloging-in-Publication Data

ISBN: 978-1-62618-766-5

Published by Nova Science Publishers, Inc. † New York

Contents

PREFACE

The imperative for the exchange of terrorism-related intelligence information among law enforcement and security officials at all levels of government is founded on three propositions. The first is that any terrorist attack in the homeland will necessarily occur in a community within a state or tribal area, and the initial response to it will be state, local, and tribal emergency responders and law enforcement officials. Second, the plotting and preparation for a terrorist attack within the United States (such as surveillance of a target, acquisition and transport of weapons or explosives, and even the recruitment of participants) will also occur within local communities. Third, "information acquired for one purpose, or under one set of authorities, might provide unique insights when combined, in accordance with applicable laws, with seemingly unrelated information for other sources." Suspicious Activity Reports (SARs) contain information about criminal activity that may also reveal terrorist pre-operational planning. Many believe that the sharing of SARs among all levels of government and the fusing of these reports with other intelligence information will help uncover terrorist plots within the United States. This book describes the Nationwide SAR Initiative (NSI), the rationale for the sharing of terrorism-related SARs, and how the NIS seeks to achieve this objective. It also examines civil liberties concerns raised by the initiative and identifies other oversight issues for Congress.

Chapter 1 – The 2004 National Commission on Terrorist Attacks Upon the United States (the 9/11 Commission) cited breakdowns in information sharing and the failure to fuse pertinent intelligence (i.e., "connecting the dots") as key factors in the failure to prevent the 9/11 attacks. Two of the efforts undertaken since 2001 to tackle these issues included

- Congress mandating the creation of an information-sharing environment (commonly known as the "ISE") that would provide and facilitate the means of sharing terrorism information among all appropriate federal, state, local, and tribal entities and the private sector through the use of policy guidelines and technologies.
- States and major urban areas establishing intelligence fusion centers to coordinate the gathering, analysis, and dissemination of law enforcement, homeland security, public safety, and terrorism intelligence and analysis.

The imperative for the exchange of terrorism-related intelligence information among law enforcement and security officials at all levels of government is founded on three propositions. The first is that any terrorist attack in the homeland will necessarily occur in a community within a state or tribal area, and the initial response to it will be by state, local, and tribal emergency responders and law enforcement officials. Second, the plotting and preparation for a terrorist attack within the United States (such as surveillance of a target, acquisition and transport of weapons or explosives, and even the recruitment of participants) will also occur within local communities. Third, "[i]nformation acquired for one purpose, or under one set of authorities, might provide unique insights when combined, in accordance with applicable law, with seemingly unrelated information from other sources."

Suspicious Activity Reports (SARs) contain information about criminal activity that may also reveal terrorist pre-operational planning. Many believe that the sharing of SARs among all levels of government and the fusing of these reports with other intelligence information will help uncover terrorist plots within the United States.

The Nationwide SAR Initiative (NSI) is an effort to have most federal, state, local, and tribal law enforcement organizations participate in a standardized, integrated approach to gathering, documenting, processing, and analyzing terrorism-related SARs. The NSI is designed to respond to the mandate of the Intelligence Reform and Terrorism Prevention Act of 2004 (P.L. 108-458), for a "decentralized, distributed, and coordinated [information sharing] environment ... with 'applicable legal standards relating to privacy and civil liberties.'"

This report describes the NSI, the rationale for the sharing of terrorism-related SARs, and how the NSI seeks to achieve this objective. It examines the privacy and civil liberties concerns raised by the initiative and identifies other oversight issues for Congress.

Chapter 2 – In 2007, DOJ and its federal partners developed the Nationwide Suspicious Activity Reporting Initiative to establish a capability to gather and share terrorism-related suspicious activity reports. GAO was asked to examine the initiative's progress and performance. This report addresses the extent to which (1) federal agencies have made progress in implementing the initiative, and what challenges, if any, remain; (2) the technical means used to collect and share reports overlap or duplicate each other; (3) training has met objectives and been completed; and (4) federal agencies are assessing the initiative's performance and results. GAO analyzed relevant documents and interviewed federal officials responsible for implementing the initiative and stakeholders from seven states (chosen based on their geographic location and other factors). The interviews are not generalizable but provided insight on progress and challenges.

Chapter 3 – The Nationwide Suspicious Activity Reporting (SAR) Initiative (NSI) Program Management Office (PMO) was established in March 2010 and is a collaborative effort led by the U.S. Department of Justice (DOJ), Bureau of Justice Assistance (BJA), in partnership with the U.S. Department of Homeland Security (DHS), the Federal Bureau of Investigation (FBI), and state, local, tribal, and territorial (SLTT) law enforcement partners. The NSI PMO has been working with the National Network of Fusion Centers, hometown security partners, and SLTT and federal law enforcement to implement the policies, processes, and standards of the NSI across all levels of government while ensuring that privacy, civil rights, and civil liberties are protected.

Over the past year, the NSI PMO has brought in new staff members who have become essential in the continued development of the NSI. The addition of the Executive Support Specialists provides law enforcement and NSI experts to the field, so they can help NSI sites with training, technical assistance, policy development and guidance, and outreach to key stakeholders and chief executives, while also ensuring that NSI sites have met all of the requirements for implementation. The NSI has worked diligently in implementing the standards, policies, and processes of the NSI across the National Network of Fusion Centers, and as of March 2012, 68 fusion centers have the capability to contribute and share suspicious activity reports, expanding the reach of the NSI to over 14,000 law enforcement agencies in 46 states, including the District of Columbia. The expansion of the NSI has allowed the Federated Search Tool to be accessed by more trained users—increasing the number of searches to more than 43,000— and over 17,000 SARs were submitted for sharing by the end of March 2011.

Since the inception of the NSI, the FBI has been a vital partner in the success of sharing terrorism-related information. Over the past year, the FBI's eGuardian team has worked closely with the NSI PMO to address and finalize issues with system compatibility, data synchronization, and alignment of policies. Through their commitment to work together, the NSI PMO and the FBI conducted outreach to the National Network of Fusion Centers to ensure that NSI sites understand the SAR reporting process, as well as the full integration of the eGuardian system and how this will help continue to improve the sharing of suspicious activity.

Launched in conjunction with the NSI, the DHS "If You See Something, Say Something™" campaign made major strides over the past year in raising public awareness of indicators related to terrorism and encouraging individuals to report suspicious activity to their local law enforcement authorities. Also, to help support the efforts of the NSI PMO, the DHS Office of Intelligence and Analysis began working to establish baseline metrics and to evaluate the analytic value of SAR information submitted to the NSI Federated Search. This will help provide support for requests for information across the divisions, as well as external state and local support requests (SLSRs), NSI-derived production of Roll Call Releases, and support to other products.

The NSI PMO has maintained a focus on reaching out to key stakeholders across the country, informing them of updates and advances to current NSI programs and training initiatives, as well as technology improvements. In the past year, the NSI Line Officer Training has been delivered to agencies and associations all over the country, and with their effort, approximately 250,000 frontline officers have reported receiving the training. With the success of the NSI Line Officer Training, the next task the NSI took on was to produce a SAR awareness training program for partners with similar missions to those of law enforcement constituencies, also referred to as hometown security partners, on behaviors and indicators of terrorist-related activity that they may come across while performing their daily responsibilities. The NSI PMO, with the assistance of subject-matter experts, developed sector-specific training for fire service and emergency medical services personnel, public safety telecommunications professionals (e.g., 9-1-1 operators), emergency managers, corrections and probation and parole officers, and private sector security personnel and those charged with protecting the nation's critical infrastructure.

Along with the development of the SAR Hometown Security Partners Training, the NSI PMO has continued to work with local law enforcement agencies on building relationships with community leaders through the

Building Communities of Trust (BCOT) initiative. This initiative focuses on developing trust among law enforcement, fusion centers, and the communities they serve, particularly immigrant and minority communities, so that crime and terrorism can be addressed. The newly published *Building Communities of Trust: A Guidance for Community Leaders* was developed in partnership with DOJ, DHS, and the International Association of Chiefs of Police (IACP) to assist community leaders in working with law enforcement agencies to facilitate dialogue and discuss ways to work together to prevent crime and terrorism.

In addition to outreach to stakeholders and the community, over the past year the NSI PMO worked with the Office of the Program Manager, Information Sharing Environment (PM-ISE); the FBI; IACP— specifically the IACP Homeland Security and Terrorism Committees—and many other key federal, state, and local representatives and law enforcement associations to develop a Unified Message that reinforces the importance of SLTT and federal entities working together to fight terrorism and help keep our communities safe. This document reiterates the importance of suspicious activity reporting and training frontline law enforcement officers so they know what behaviors and indicators to look for while still ensuring privacy, civil rights, and civil liberties protections when they do. This message also underscores the importance of the sharing of SAR information with the FBI's Joint Terrorism Task Forces (JTTFs) for further investigation and with state and major urban area fusion centers (fusion centers) for analysis. The Unified Message also reinforces the important role local communities play and encourages them to work together with DHS on the "If You See Something, Say Something™" campaign, which raises public awareness of behavioral indicators of terrorism and emphasizes the importance of the public in reporting suspicious activities to local law enforcement.

Over the past year, the NSI PMO made a number of technology improvements to the NSI Federated Search and has also provided resources to assist users, if needed. These new modifications include a Single Line Search, similar to a Google search; a subscription service, where users can create and save queries; a new NSI Analytical Tool that will allow users to review specific information easily; and also a Help Desk and Frequently Asked Questions (FAQs) site, where users will find useful information pertaining to the NSI program.

Chapter 4 – This status report on the Nationwide Suspicious Activity Reporting (SAR) Initiative (NSI) provides a summary assessment of the ISE-SAR Evaluation Environment over the last two years, highlighting four key findings and identifying a number of valuable lessons- learned. The report also provides specific recommendations to help guide the broader NSI implementation as it begins in 2010.

Over the last two years, federal, state, and local organizations have developed, tested, and evaluated the policies, procedures, and technology concepts needed to implement a unified process for gathering, documenting, processing, analyzing, and sharing suspicious activity reports that are determined to be reasonably indicative of criminal activity associated with terrorism. The Evaluation Environment provided a controlled environment where agencies could evaluate potential solutions to operational challenges and identify best practices to be incorporated as part of a broader nationwide implementation. Although the Evaluation Environment period drew to a close at the end of Fiscal Year 2009, the operational process established at the participating agencies remains in place and sites continue to share ISE-SARs on a regular basis as part of the NSI. Additional sites are already being incorporated into the process even as the plans for a full nationwide implementation are developed.

This report provides an overview of the results of the Evaluation Environment as of November 2009. In addition, two related reports will be issued in early 2010:

1. The Program Manager for the Information Sharing Environment (PM-ISE)—in consultation with the Civil Liberties and Privacy Office of the Director of National Intelligence (DNI), the Office of Privacy and Civil Liberties of the Department of Justice (DOJ), and the Legal Issues Working Group of the ISE Privacy Guidelines Committee (PGC)—is preparing an updated *NSI Privacy, Civil rights, and Civil Liberties Analysis* that provides a more detailed view of this critical aspect of NSI implementation, and
2. The PM-ISE and the DOJ Bureau of Justice Assistance (BJA), with input from state and local law enforcement, fusion center personnel, and community advocates, are developing guidance for local law enforcement and fusion centers on developing trust relationships with community representatives based on the lessons-learned from the *Building Communities of Trust* initiative. This initiative aims to build bridges and mutual understanding among community groups, local law enforcement agencies, and state and major urban area fusion centers as a way of better protecting our local communities. The outcome is for law enforcement officers, public safety personnel,

community leaders, and citizens to be better able to distinguish between innocent cultural behaviors and behavior indicative of criminal activity; and for local communities to play a more supportive role in combating terrorism-related crime. This effort is discussed in more detail in the Lessons-Learned section of this report.

In: Nationwide Suspicious Activity … ISBN: 978-1-62618-766-5
Editor: Laurits Hartmann © 2013 Nova Science Publishers, Inc.

Chapter 1

TERRORISM INFORMATION SHARING AND THE NATIONWIDE SUSPICIOUS ACTIVITY REPORT INITIATIVE: BACKGROUND AND ISSUES FOR CONGRESS*

Jerome P. Bjelopera

SUMMARY

The 2004 National Commission on Terrorist Attacks Upon the United States (the 9/11 Commission) cited breakdowns in information sharing and the failure to fuse pertinent intelligence (i.e., "connecting the dots") as key factors in the failure to prevent the 9/11 attacks. Two of the efforts undertaken since 2001 to tackle these issues included

- Congress mandating the creation of an information-sharing environment (commonly known as the "ISE") that would provide and facilitate the means of sharing terrorism information among all appropriate federal, state, local, and tribal entities and the private sector through the use of policy guidelines and technologies.

* This is an edited, reformatted and augmented version of the Congressional Research Service Publication, CRS Report for Congress R40901, dated December 28, 2011.

- States and major urban areas establishing intelligence fusion centers to coordinate the gathering, analysis, and dissemination of law enforcement, homeland security, public safety, and terrorism intelligence and analysis.

The imperative for the exchange of terrorism-related intelligence information among law enforcement and security officials at all levels of government is founded on three propositions.

The first is that any terrorist attack in the homeland will necessarily occur in a community within a state or tribal area, and the initial response to it will be by state, local, and tribal emergency responders and law enforcement officials.

Second, the plotting and preparation for a terrorist attack within the United States (such as surveillance of a target, acquisition and transport of weapons or explosives, and even the recruitment of participants) will also occur within local communities.

Third, "[i]nformation acquired for one purpose, or under one set of authorities, might provide unique insights when combined, in accordance with applicable law, with seemingly unrelated information from other sources."

Suspicious Activity Reports (SARs) contain information about criminal activity that may also reveal terrorist pre-operational planning. Many believe that the sharing of SARs among all levels of government and the fusing of these reports with other intelligence information will help uncover terrorist plots within the United States.

The Nationwide SAR Initiative (NSI) is an effort to have most federal, state, local, and tribal law enforcement organizations participate in a standardized, integrated approach to gathering, documenting, processing, and analyzing terrorism-related SARs. The NSI is designed to respond to the mandate of the Intelligence Reform and Terrorism Prevention Act of 2004 (P.L. 108-458), for a "decentralized, distributed, and coordinated [information sharing] environment ... with 'applicable legal standards relating to privacy and civil liberties.'"

This report describes the NSI, the rationale for the sharing of terrorism-related SARs, and how the NSI seeks to achieve this objective. It examines the privacy and civil liberties concerns raised by the initiative and identifies other oversight issues for Congress.

BACKGROUND

The National Commission on Terrorist Attacks Upon the United States (the 9/11 Commission) cited breakdowns in information sharing and the failure to fuse pertinent intelligence (i.e., "connecting the dots") as key factors in the failure to prevent the 9/11 attacks.[1] A bipartisan task force[2] of former policy makers and senior executives described the challenge facing the government in "the new era of national security we have entered," as "the challenge of using information effectively, linking collection with sound and imaginative analysis derived from multiple perspectives, and employing cutting edge technology to support end-users, from emergency responders to Presidents. In other words, we need to *mobilize* information."[3]

In the 2004 Intelligence Reform and Terrorism Prevention Act (IRTPA), Congress mandated the creation of an Information Sharing Environment (commonly known as the "ISE").[4] Congress intended the ISE to be a "decentralized, distributed, and coordinated environment ... with 'applicable legal standards relating to privacy and civil liberties.'" The act also directed that the ISE provide and facilitate the means of sharing terrorism information among all appropriate federal, state, local, and tribal entities and the private sector through the use of policy guidelines and technologies.[5]

A Program Manager for the Information Sharing Environment (PM-ISE) was established and placed within the Office of the Director of National Intelligence (ODNI). As required by Section 1016(h) of the IRTPA, the PM-ISE submitted to Congress three annual reports on the extent to which the ISE has been implemented.[6] The Obama Administration reaffirmed effective information sharing as a "top priority" and established within the Executive Office of the President the position of Senior Director for Information Sharing Policy.[7]

Also after 9/11, states and major urban areas established intelligence fusion centers to coordinate the gathering, analysis, and dissemination of law enforcement, homeland security, public safety, and terrorism intelligence and analysis.[8] According to the Department of Homeland Security (DHS), this activity by fusion centers contributes to the ISE.[9] Fusion centers have been defined as a "collaborative effort of two or more Federal, state, local, or tribal government agencies that combines resources, expertise, or information with the goal of maximizing the ability of such agencies to detect, prevent, investigate, apprehend, and respond to criminal or terrorist activity."[10] As of December 2011, DHS notes that 72 centers are operational within the United

States and its territories.[11] DHS has supported these centers with grant funding and has assigned intelligence officers to them.[12]

Why Information Sharing?

> Information sharing is ... about establishing a collaborative environment with a clear purpose: ensuring that the right people have access to the right information at the right time under the right conditions to enable informed decisions.[13]

The imperative for the exchange of terrorism-related intelligence information among law enforcement and security officials at all levels of government is founded on three propositions.

The first is that any terrorist attack in the homeland will necessarily occur in a community within a state or tribal area, and the initial response to it will be by state, local, and tribal emergency responders and law enforcement officials.

Second, the plotting and preparation for a terrorist attack within the United States (such as surveillance of a target, acquisition and transport of weapons or explosives, and even the recruitment of participants) will also occur within communities. Every day, officers at thousands of state and local law enforcement agencies collect and document information regarding behaviors, incidents, and other suspicious activity associated with crime including terrorism.[14] A joint study by the Departments of Justice and Homeland Security and senior law enforcement officials concluded that "[t]he gathering, processing, reporting, analyzing, and sharing of suspicious activity is critical to preventing crimes, including those associated with domestic and international terrorism."[15]

Third, "[i]nformation acquired for one purpose, or under one set of authorities, might provide unique insights when combined, in accordance with applicable law, with seemingly unrelated information from other sources."[16] This recognizes that "relevant information comes from a much wider range of sources … and it is difficult to know *a priori* what information will prove relevant to analysts or useful to users. For this reason, it is necessary to create a more horizontal, cooperative, and fluid process for intelligence collection, sharing, and analysis."[17] Or, as the 9/11 Commission concluded, "A 'smart' government would *integrate* all sources of information to see the enemy as a whole."[18]

Information-Sharing Systems

In a nationwide survey conducted in 2006, the Justice Research and Statistics Association (JRSA) found that there are currently in place or under development 266 separate systems that share information about crime, including terrorism, at the national, regional, and state levels.[19] The boom in the development of these systems has led to concern that "it is hard to know what information is being shared and who is sharing it. In many cases, multiple systems are being developed to cover overlapping areas."[20] **Appendix A** provides a brief overview of significant information-sharing systems.

SUSPICIOUS ACTIVITY REPORTING

Suspicious Activity Reports (SAR) contain information about criminal activity that may also reveal terrorist pre-operational planning.[21] These reports could be based on an officer's observation of suspicious behavior, 9-1-1 calls, or other tips and leads provided to police by citizens. Many believe that the sharing of SARs among all levels of government and combining them with other intelligence information will help uncover terrorist plots within the United States. Every day, more than 800,000 police officers collect and document information regarding behaviors, incidents, and other suspicious activity associated with crime, including terrorism.

"On the beat or mobile, cops are sensitive to things that do not look right or do not sound right," says one police chief. "[R]emember, it was a rookie cop on a routine check that resulted in the arrest of Eric Robert Rudolph in North Carolina despite the enormous commitment of federal resources."[22] Oklahoma City bomber Timothy McVeigh was arrested after a traffic stop when Oklahoma State Trooper Charles J. Hanger noticed that McVeigh's yellow 1977 Mercury Marquis had no license plate.[23] Using his home state as an example, a former U.S. Attorney maintains that "evidence of a potential terrorist threat or organized criminal enterprise is far more likely to be found in the incidental contact with the 10,000 police officers in the state of Washington than by the less than 150 FBI agents assigned to the Seattle Field Division."[24]

In addition to the arrests of Rudolph and McVeigh, state and local law enforcement officers, in the normal course of their duties, have uncovered or disrupted the following terrorist plots:

- The Japanese Red Army terrorist, Yū Kikumura, was arrested on April 12, 1988, at a rest stop on the New Jersey Turnpike by a state trooper who thought he was acting suspiciously. He was found carrying three 18-inch (46-cm) pipe bombs loaded with gunpowder. Prosecutors said Kikumura had planned to bomb a military recruitment office in New York City.[25]
- In July 2005, two undercover police officers noticed two men acting suspiciously near a gas station in Torrance, CA. After the men robbed the gas station, they were arrested by the undercover officers. A search of the arrested men's apartment revealed that they were members of the terrorist group Jamiyyat Ul-Islan Is-Saheeh. They were planning to bomb synagogues in Los Angeles and were financing their operation through armed robberies.[26]
- In August 4, 2007, two Egyptians studying in Florida were stopped by police for a traffic violation near Goose Creek, SC. They were found to have explosives in their vehicle. A subsequent investigation revealed that one of the students had made and placed on the Internet a video demonstrating how to use a doll to conceal an improvised explosive device. The student later plead guilty to "providing material support to terrorism."[27]

One major city police department commander notes that the role of police officers has evolved after 9/11. They are now also "first preventers" of terrorism, and this represents a "dramatic paradigm shift," both for the federal government and for the local and state agencies themselves.[28] The need for intelligence information to support the police in this terrorism prevention role is considered crucial.[29]

A national information-sharing system, says a former U.S. Attorney, should also ensure that "federal agencies have access to information maintained in state and local agencies that may be pertinent to terrorist threats ... the benefit that would accrue to U.S. national security in having police records integrated in a strictly controlled fashion with sensitive federal data would be nothing short of remarkable."[30] He cites the example of Hani Hanjoor, the hijacker who piloted American Airlines Flight 77 that crashed into the Pentagon. Six weeks prior to the 9/11 attacks, Hanjoor had been issued a speeding ticket by a local police department in the Washington, DC, area. Had a system been in place to share this information with the FBI, it may have alerted them that a suspected Al Qaeda operative was present within the National Capital Region. Also prior to September 11, 2001, local police officers made separate traffic stops of two other 9/11 hijackers—Mohammed Atta and Ziad Samir Jarrah. Like Hanjoor, both were in violation of their immigration status. There was even an outstanding arrest warrant on Atta for failing to appear on a previous traffic citation.[31]

NATIONWIDE SUSPICIOUS ACTIVITY REPORTING INITIATIVE (NSI)

The NSI is a framework to support the reporting of suspicious activity—from the point of initial observation to the point where the information is available in the information-sharing environment.[32] It supports one of the core principles of the 2007 *National Strategy for Information Sharing*, that information sharing "be woven into all aspects of the counterterrorism activity, including preventive and protective actions, actionable responses, criminal and counterterrorism investigative activities, event preparedness, and response to and recovery from catastrophic events."[33] The NSI responds to the strategy's mandate that the federal government support the development of a nationwide capacity for a standardized, integrated approach to gathering, documenting, processing, analyzing, and sharing information about suspicious activity that is potentially terrorism-related while protecting the privacy and civil liberties of Americans.[34]

According to the PM-ISE, the NSI is neither a technology nor a single, monolithic program. Rather it is a coordinated effort that integrates all SAR-related activities into a nationwide unified process.[35] The NSI is a framework that defines the data standards, business processes, and policies that facilitate the sharing of terrorism-related SARs. NSI has been described as

> a partnership among federal, state, local, tribal, and territorial law enforcement that establishes a national capacity for gathering, documenting, processing, analyzing, and sharing SAR information—also referred to as the SAR process—in a manner that rigorously protects the privacy and civil liberties of Americans.[36]

According to the 2010 *Nationwide SAR Initiative Annual Report,* 29 fusion centers had implemented the NSI process and achieved operational status, with another 30 fusion centers in progress as of March 2011.[37]

The NSI also differs from data mining programs. Data mining entails the search of numerous commercial or government data sets that contain data—the vast majority of which documents legal activity. Mathematical algorithms are then used to identify data trends that can be examined as predictors of criminal activity. The NSI establishes a federated search[38] capability that requires the articulation of some type of criminal or law enforcement predicate before permitting a search of repositories consisting of documented events that are themselves considered reasonably indicative of criminal activity. Given the controversies surrounding various data mining programs,[39] this difference may be a salient issue in terms of public acceptance of the NSI program.

In December 2008, a concept of operations for the NSI program was published that describes the roles, missions, and responsibilities of NSI participating agencies and the top level NSI governing structure.[40] A comprehensive overview of the operational steps of the nationwide SAR cycle grouped into five business process activities—planning, gathering and processing, analysis and production, dissemination, and reevaluation—is shown in **Figure 1**.

The intended operational steps of the cycle can be described simply: When a police officer detects suspicious activity that might be terrorist related, he or she documents that activity in a SAR. That report is reviewed within the officer's chain of command. Once vetted, it is submitted to a state/local fusion center, where it is reviewed by a trained intelligence analyst to determine whether it meets the established SAR criteria.[41] If so, the report is entered into the information-sharing environment, where it becomes accessible to authorized agencies at all levels of government and available for analysis and fusion with other intelligence information.[42]

Privacy and Civil Liberties Implications

According to the commander responsible for the Los Angeles Police Department (LAPD) SAR program, a suspicious activity reporting program should be "built upon behaviors and activities that have been historically linked to preoperational planning and preparation for terrorist attacks." Appropriately managed, a SAR program "takes the emphasis off the racial or ethnic characteristics of individuals and places it on detecting behaviors and activities with potential links to terrorism related criminal activity."[43]

Some observers, however, are concerned that many behaviors that the police observe, and then use to judge whether the behaviors might be precursors to terrorism, are often entirely innocent and perfectly legal.

Consider the following behaviors derived from the LAPD list of SAR "suspect actions":[44]

- Uses binoculars or cameras.
- Takes measurements.
- Takes pictures or video footage.
- Draws diagrams or takes notes.
- Pursues specific training or education that indicate suspicious motives (flight training, weapons training, etc).
- Espouses extremist views.

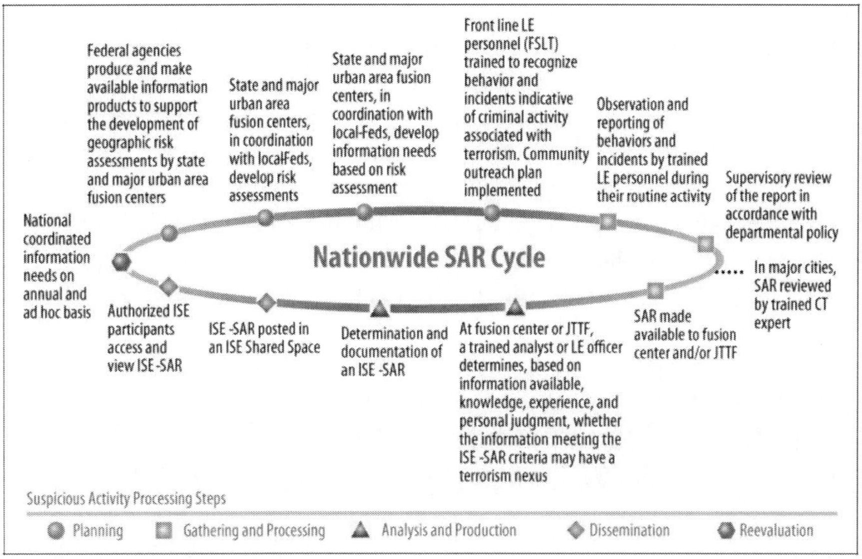

Source: PM-ISE, *Information Sharing Environment (ISE), Functional Standard (FS) Suspicious Activity Reporting (SAR), Version 1.5,* May 21, 2009, p. 8, http://www.dhs.gov/xlibrary/assets/privacy/privacy-pia-dhswide-sar-ise-appendix.pdf.

Figure 1. Nationwide Suspicious Activity Reporting (SAR) Cycle.

The American Civil Liberties Union (ACLU) argues that "[m]ost people engage in one or more of these activities on a routine, if not daily, basis." They fear that "overbroad reporting authority gives law enforcement officers justification to harass practically anyone they choose, to collect personal information, and to pass such information along to the intelligence community."[45] The Center for Democracy and Technology (CDT) is concerned that "there is a trend toward the collection of huge quantities of information with little or no predicate through SARs. There seems to us a high risk that this information will be misinterpreted and used to the detriment of innocent persons."[46]

In support of this contention, both the ACLU and CDT cite a case reported by the *Baltimore Sun* in July 2008: "Undercover Maryland State Police officers [in 2005 and 2006] ... sent covert agents to infiltrate the Baltimore Pledge of Resistance, a peace group; the Baltimore Coalition Against the Death Penalty; and the Committee to Save Vernon Evans, a death row inmate."[47] The police "also entered the names of some in a law-enforcement database of people thought to be terrorists or drug traffickers." According to files obtained by the ACLU through a Maryland Information Act lawsuit, "none of the 43 pages of summaries and computer logs—some with agents' names and whole paragraphs blacked out—mention criminal or even potentially criminal acts, the legal standard for initiating such surveillance."[48]

A challenge for the NSI is how to achieve law enforcement and intelligence objectives while ensuring privacy and civil liberties protections for American citizens. For example, all of the behaviors listed by the LAPD could be potential indicators of terrorist planning and preparation. But such behaviors could also be innocent and legal activities. Carefully articulating what activity crosses the threshold into reportable suspicious activity is seen as a necessary step to ensuring the protection of privacy and civil liberties.

The NSI has endeavored to address these issues. Agencies participating in the NSI are required to implement a privacy policy that is at least as comprehensive as the policy elaborated within the ISE Privacy Guidelines[49] and that includes a SAR provision.[50] Likewise, all fusion centers have similar protections.[51]

ISE SAR Functional Standard

Also in an effort to address civil liberties issues associated with the NSI, the PM ISE published a *ISE SAR Functional Standard*, which describes the structure, content, and products associated with processing, integrating, and retrieving SARs by participating agencies.[52] It is specifically intended to establish a structured environment to reduce inappropriate police data gathering and support the training of law enforcement personnel so that they can better distinguish between behavior that is legal or constitutionally protected and that which is potentially associated with criminal activity. It establishes threshold criteria for what suspicious activity will be considered as having a nexus to terrorism and establishes a process to determine whether reports of that activity meet the criteria for being entered into the ISE as a SAR. The 2010 *Nationwide SAR Initiative Annual Report* states:

> The current ISE-SAR Functional Standard reinforces constitutional standards, including the protection of rights guaranteed by the First Amendment and limitations on the use of certain factors—race, ethnicity, national origin, or religious affiliation—in the gathering, collecting, storing, and sharing of information about individuals. As a result of input from privacy advocates, the standard also includes reliability indicators. Through the use of Information Exchange Package Documentation ... the Functional Standard allows the originating agency to include or not include fields that contain personal information, based upon the agency's rules and policies.[53]

In 2008, the PM ISE completed a report that examined the potential impact of the *ISE SAR Functional Standard* on the privacy and other legal rights of Americans, how it will be evaluated in a limited operational environment, and articulated the measures that will be established to protect privacy and civil liberties.[54]

Subsequently, the Office of the PM-ISE engaged with various stakeholders, including privacy and civil liberties groups such as the ACLU, CDT, and the Freedom and Justice Foundation, as it developed and refined SAR-related operational processes and training.[55] In May 2009, the suggestions of these groups as well as state and local law enforcement agencies were incorporated into a revised version of the *ISE SAR Functional Standard.*[56] Among the changes in the revision (Version 1.5) were the following:[57]

- Refines the definition of "suspicious activity," as "observed behavior reasonably indicative of pre-operational planning related to terrorism or other criminal activity."
- Further emphasizes a behavior-focused approach to identify suspicious activity and requires that factors such as race, ethnicity, national origin, or religious affiliation should not be considered factors that create suspicion.
- Refines the guidance to distinguish between Defined Criminal Activity and Potentially Criminal or Non-Criminal Activity requiring additional factual information before investigation.

- Clarifies those activities that are generally First Amendment-protected and should not be reported in a SAR absent articulable facts and circumstances that support the source agency's suspicion that the behavior observed is reasonably indicative of criminal activity associated with terrorism.

In a press release following publication of Version 1.5, the ACLU National Security Policy Counsel noted that

> [t]he revised guidelines for suspicious activity reporting establish that a reasonable connection to terrorism or other criminal activity is required before law enforcement may collect Americans' personal information and share it within the ISE. These changes to the standard, which include reiterating that race cannot be used as a factor to create suspicion, give law enforcement the authority it needs without sacrificing the rights of those it seeks to protect.[58]

To bolster these efforts, NSI PMO developed the document "Vetting ISE-SAR Data: A Pathway to Ensure Best Practices." It articulates guidance for fusion center analysts on how to vet SAR information, provides compliance with the ISE-SAR Functional Standard v. 1.5.[59]

Also, according to the PM-ISE, for reported activity to make its way into a SAR, the activity "must conform to one or more of the criteria identified in Part B of the ISE-SAR Functional Standard."[60]

Community Outreach

Two projects related to community outreach and associated with the NSI have emerged. These have endeavored to connect private citizens to the SAR process.[61]

Building Communities of Trust Initiative (BCOT)

In recognition that NSI's success depends on partnership with local communities, the Building Communities of Trust Initiative (BCOT) was developed by DOJ and DHS. It resulted in guidance for the development of trust among three sets of actors—fusion centers, law enforcement, and the communities in which they operate.[62] All of these actors have a stake in the production of SARs. These recommendations included items such as

- training of fusion center analysts in cultural sensitivity so that they can distinguish behavior that is constitutionally protected from criminal or terrorist activity;
- encouraging law enforcement to "embrace" community policing by "emphasizing partnerships and problem solving"; and
- encouraging communities to view information sharing with fusion centers and law enforcement as key to crime prevention and counterterrorism.[63]

"If You See Something, Say Something™" Campaign

In July 2010, DHS launched its national "If You See Something, Say Something™" campaign. It is meant to "raise public awareness of indicators of terrorism and terrorism-related crime and to emphasize the importance of reporting suspicious activity to the proper transportation and law enforcement authorities."[64] DHS has tied the campaign to NSI as a way of emphasizing community awareness regarding terrorism.[65]

NSI Shared Space Architecture

NSI participants can make their SARs available within the NSI federated search via two methods. They can install "an NSI-provided server that leverages an existing legacy computer-aided dispatch … system or records management system…."

Alternatively, they can create an *eGuardian* account to disseminate SARs.[66] Via this architecture, law enforcement agencies can share information without having to open up their own internal databases to outside users. Simultaneously, law enforcement agencies control their own information and determine what they want to share.[67]

This shared space architecture also allows participants to search existing SARs via the NSI Federated Search. NSI participants can access the NSI Federated Search through either the Regional Information Sharing Systems® Secure Intranet (RISSNET™) or Law Enforcement Online (LEO). Eventually, participants will be able to access the search through the Homeland Security Information Network portal geared toward law enforcement.[68] The Federated Search is represented as the "Entry point into ISE Shared Spaces Environment" in Figure 2.

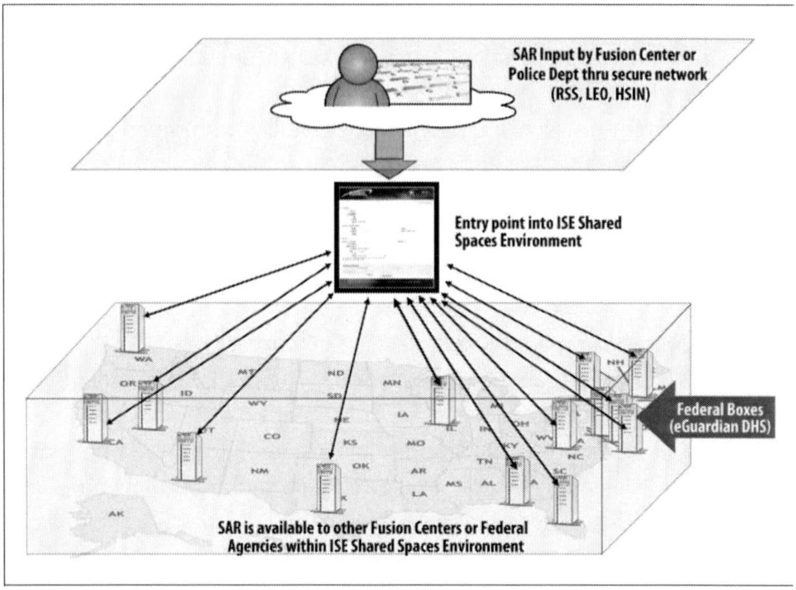

Source: DOJ, Bureau of Justice Assistance.

Figure 2. ISE SAR "Shared Space" Concept.

The FBI's *eGuardian* system[69] is a node within the ISE Shared Spaces environment. On the surface, it would appear that the existing *eGuardian* capability duplicates the NSI—or at least NSI's shared spaces concept. But it should be noted that the NSI is an overall framework for a SAR process that includes policies, governance, procedures, training, and information technology (IT) architecture, whereas *eGuardian* is a specific technology for terrorism-related information sharing.[70]

Under NSI, *eGuardian* can remain the technology that FBI uses to supply data to and access data from the ISE Shared Spaces environment. Likewise, fusion centers or state and local governments may, if they wish, use *eGuardian* as a gateway to and from the shared spaces. However, some law enforcement agencies may choose, or are legislatively mandated, to maintain a repository of their own data and to control what data is shared with whom based on statutory criteria. Consistent with the requirement in the IRTPA for a "decentralized, distributed, and coordinated" information-sharing environment, the NSI shared spaces architecture allows state, local, and tribal agencies to maintain control of their own data.[71]

Training

The training regimen that has been established for the NSI has three levels. At one level, the SAR process training involves briefings for law enforcement executives regarding "executive leadership, policy development, privacy and civil liberties protections, agency training, and community outreach."[72] Another level—the SAR Analytic Role Training—is directed at those involved in analyzing SAR information, "ensuring that SARs are properly reviewed and vetted is critical to promoting the integrity of information submitted; protecting citizens' privacy, civil rights, and civil liberties; and successfully implementing the SAR process."[73] The analytic training revolves around teaching analysts and investigators "to recognize terrorism-related pre-incident indicators and to validate—based on a combination of knowledge, experience, and available information—whether the behavior has a potential nexus to terrorism and meets criteria for submission."[74] The final level—Line Officer Trainingυfocuses on frontline law enforcement personnel. They are trained to "recognize behavior and incidents that may indicate criminal activity associated with terrorism."[75] As of October 2011, more than 160,000 law enforcement officers received SAR training.[76] According to the 2010 *Nationwide SAR Initiative Annual Report*, training for two additional groups is also necessary. The first of these groups includes public safety/justice professionals involved in fire service, emergency medical service, emergency management, and corrections, as well as probation and parole officers. The second group consists of private-sector owners, operators, and protectors of critical infrastructure.[77]

The NSI Pilot Project

In 2007, the Office of the PM-ISE funded a pilot effort called the "ISE-SAR Evaluation Environment" (ISE-SAR EE) to evaluate the feasibility of the NSI for the sharing of terrorism-related SARs.[78] Program management services for the project were provided by DOJ's Bureau of Justice Assistance (BJA)[79] with the support of the Global Justice Information Sharing Initiative.[80]

The ISE-SAR EE sought to develop and implement consistent national policies, processes, and best practices among the federal, state, local, and tribal partners in the NSI initiative. System evaluations and training activities were conducted at three state and nine urban fusion center pilot sites.[81] That evaluation program concluded on September 30, 2009. There were two specific activities of note within the ISE-SAR EE. First, the project team furnished and tested the "shared spaces" concept. Second, a pilot training program was developed for the thousands of state and local law enforcement officers to assist them in the detection, identification, and reporting of suspicious activity in a way that supports the analysis and fusion of such reports into actionable intelligence while protecting privacy and civil liberties.

ISE-SAR EE Final Report Key Recommendations

In January 2010, the final report of the ISE-SAR EE[82] provided a number of key recommendations. These include securing the support of executive leadership within agencies involved in the SAR process.[83] According to the final report, agencies should form their own unique policies and procedures regarding SARs while folding in a common set of processes across participating agencies. Agencies should maintain privacy frameworks consistent with the ISE Privacy Guidelines.[84] The final report also emphasizes the importance of effectively deploying technology, of offering training, and of outreach to build public, private sector, and law enforcement awareness of the SAR process.[85]

Formation of a Program Management Office

In March 2010, a Program Management Office (PMO) was established within the BJA "to facilitate the implementation of the NSI across all levels of government."[86] The PMO's purpose is largely to "assist agencies with adopting compatible processes, policies, and standards that foster broader sharing of SARs, while ensuring that privacy, civil rights, and civil liberties are protected."[87] The PMO plays an advocacy role for the NSI. It guides participating agencies at all levels and also coordinates NSI efforts. The PMO has also highlighted the importance of privacy and civil liberties issues by working with the DOJ Privacy and Civil Liberties Office.[88]

Issues for Congress

Too Many "Dots"

The NSI is designed to increase the amount of information—the intelligence "dots"—that will flow from state, local, and tribal law enforcement agencies to the federal government. The goal of "connecting the dots" becomes more difficult when there is an increasingly large volume of "dots" to sift through and analyze. Because the NSI would establish mechanisms for—and indeed promote—the widespread reporting and sharing of data by numerous federal, state, and local agencies, some have expressed concerns about the risk of "'pipe clogging' as huge amounts of information are ... gathered without apparent focus."[89]

In an October 2007 report,[90] the Government Accountability Office (GAO) identified a related challenge. When "identical or similar types of information are collected by or submitted to multiple agencies, integrating or sharing this information can lead to redundancies." The GAO found "that in intelligence fusion centers, multiple information systems created redundancies of information that made it difficult to discern what was relevant. As a result, end users were overwhelmed with duplicative information from multiple sources."[91]

A challenge for the NSI is the extent to which the program will result in an avalanche of largely irrelevant or duplicative data while diverting the police from more productive law enforcement activities. For example, in a 40-month period before the ISE-SAR EE pilot program, the FBI documented approximately 108,000 potential terrorism-related threats, reports of suspicious incidents, and terrorist watchlist encounters.[92]

Congress may be interested in how a future SAR Program Management Office intends to address this problem—specifically, which agency or agencies will be responsible for quality control of SARs to prevent system overload from irrelevant or redundant ones and to ensure that the SARs that are entered into the shared space environment adhere to privacy and civil liberties standards.

Data Privacy and Access

To achieve information-sharing objectives, government agency partners need to establish wide-scale electronic trust between the caretakers of sensitive information and those who need and are authorized to use that information.[93] The Markle Task Force on National Security in the Information Age, maintains that

> [i]n an effective information sharing framework, information is not simply shared without restraint ... information sharing will succeed only

if accompanied by government-wide policy guidelines and oversight to provide robust protections for privacy and civil liberties ... [i]ts governance should require a user to provide a predicate in order to access data under an authorized use standard. To establish a predicate, an analyst seeking information would need to state a mission- or threat-based need to access the information for a particular purpose."[94]

To accomplish this, proponents say that fusion centers must acquire a federated capability for identity and privilege management that securely communicates a user's roles, rights, and privileges to ensure network security and privacy protections. The two elements of this are identification/authentication—the identity of end users and how they were authenticated—and privilege management—the certifications, clearances, job functions, and organizational affiliations associated with end users that serve as the basis for authorization decisions.[95]

In order to protect sensitive data and the privacy of Americans, Congress may wish to examine the NSI policies that will govern data privacy and access to data within the ISE Shared Spaces environment.

Information Technology (IT) Infrastructure

The success of the NSI is dependent on an IT infrastructure that enables state and local fusion centers to have access to each other's information as well as to the appropriate federal databases. Under the "shared space architecture" concept, fusion centers replicate data from their systems to an external server under their control.

A secure portal is then created that allows simultaneous searching of all such databases so that fusion centers will be able to aggregate any relevant information that exists throughout the network. To connect into the system, a fusion center requires a server and software to translate data from whatever case management or intelligence system it uses to a separate database on the server.

Expenses for this IT infrastructure may exceed the funds that states and cities will allocate for their fusion centers from the State Homeland Security Program (SHSP) or Urban Area Security Initiative (UASI). Congress may wish to consider ways to provide funding to fusion centers for this purpose.

Metrics

One of the biggest challenges facing policy makers is how to determine whether the NSI program is successful:

- Are the number of SARs produced or the number of SARs shared relevant metrics?
- How does one know if the SARs that are produced and shared under the program are actually meaningful intelligence "dots?"
- How does one determine if the right "dots" are being connected?

Congress may wish to ask the NSI PMO about metrics to measure the success of the NSI program.

APPENDIX A. SIGNIFICANT INFORMATION-SHARING SYSTEMS

Law Enforcement Online (LEO)

Established prior to the 9/11 attacks, LEO is a secure, Internet-based communications portal for law enforcement, first responders, criminal justice professionals, and anti-terrorism and intelligence agencies around the globe. Managed by the FBI's Criminal Justice Information Services Division, LEO catalyzes and strengthens collaboration and information-sharing by providing access to sensitive but unclassified information and various state-of-the-art communications services and tools. It is available around the clock and is offered free of charge to members of the criminal justice and intelligence communities, as well as military and government agencies associated with infrastructure protection in the United States.[96]

Regional Information Sharing Systems Program (RISS)

Also established prior to the 9/11 attacks, RISS is a national network of six multistate centers designed to operate on a regional basis. It is federally funded and administered by DOJ's Bureau of Justice Assistance (BJA). RISS supports law enforcement efforts nationwide to combat illegal drug trafficking, identity theft, human trafficking, violent crime, and terrorist activity, and to promote officer safety. The regional centers provide member law enforcement agencies with a broad range of intelligence exchange and related investigative support services. RISS operates a secure intranet, known as RISSNET™, to facilitate law enforcement communications and information sharing nationwide.[97]

Homeland Security Information Network (HSIN)

After the 9/11 attacks, DHS established the HSIN, a secured, Web-based platform for sensitive but unclassified information sharing and collaboration between federal, state, local, tribal, private sector, and international partners. The HSIN platform was created to interface with existing information-sharing networks to support the diverse communities of interest engaged in preventing, protecting from, responding to, and recovering from all threats, hazards, and incidents under the jurisdiction of DHS. There are five community of interest portals on HSIN: Emergency Management, Critical Sectors, Law Enforcement, Multi-Mission Agencies, and Intelligence and Analysis. HSIN provides real-time, interactive connectivity between states and major urban areas and the 24/7 DHS operations center—the National Operations Center (NOC).[98]

The HSIN-Intelligence portal provides state, local, and tribal officials with access to unclassified intelligence products. Classified intelligence products are provided to state and local fusion centers that have the appropriate security infrastructure through the Homeland Security Data Network (HSDN). Through HSDN, users can access collateral Secret-level terrorism-related information including products from the National Counterterrorism Center's (NCTC) *NCTC Online*.

Law Enforcement Information Sharing Program (LEISP)

After 9/11, DOJ initiated the LEISP to foster the sharing of information across jurisdictional boundaries to prevent terrorism and to systematically improve the investigation and prosecution of criminal activity.[99] Two significant systems under the LEISP are described below:[100]

OneDOJ System

This system is a repository of data from DOJ law enforcement components (Bureau of Alcohol, Tobacco, Firearms, and Explosives; Bureau of Prisons; Drug Enforcement Administration; FBI; and the U.S. Marshals Service) that enables the sharing of investigative information within the department. It is hosted at the FBI's Criminal Justice Information Services (CJIS) data center. External sharing is accomplished through bilateral partnerships with designated regional, state, or federal sharing initiatives. These partnerships allow non-DOJ users to access OneDOJ data from within their own systems and vice-versa. However, data are not contributed by external partners to the OneDOJ system.

Law Enforcement National Data Exchange (N-DEx)

N-DEx is intended to facilitate the sharing of information across jurisdictional boundaries and to provide new investigative tools that enhance the nation's ability to fight crime and terrorism. Its proposed services and capabilities would allow participating agencies to detect relationships between people, places, things, and crime characteristics; to link information across jurisdictions; and to "connect the dots" between apparently unrelated data without causing information overload.

FBI Terrorist Threat Information Tracking Systems

After 9/11, the FBI established two programs for the tracking, analysis, and sharing of information about terrorism threats:

Guardian

Guardian is described as a classified information technology system that allows the FBI to collect and review reports of suspicious activity in an organized way to determine which ones warrant additional investigative follow-up.[101] The primary purpose is not to manage cases, but to facilitate the reporting, tracking, and management of threats to determine within a short time span whether a particular matter should be closed or referred for an investigation. Guardian's database can be searched by FBI employees and certain other government agency partners thus providing a capability to analyze threat information for trends and patterns.[102]

eGuardian

A companion system to Guardian is *eGuardian*. It is an unclassified system designed to enable near real-time sharing and tracking of terrorist information and suspicious activity with federal, state, local, and tribal agencies.[103] Unclassified information from the Guardian system that appears to have a potential nexus to terrorism is to be passed down to *eGuardian*, where it will be available for viewing by those members of state, local, and tribal law enforcement and representatives of other federal law enforcement agencies that have been given permission to access the system.[104] It is also intended to serve as the mechanism for the electronic transmittal of leads by state, local, and tribal agencies to the JTTF's. FBI has made *eGuardian* available on its secure LEO Internet portal, allowing more than 18,000 agencies to run searches and input their own reports.

APPENDIX B. ACRONYMS USED IN THIS REPORT

ACLU	American Civil Liberties Union
BCOT	Building Communities of Trust Initiative
BJA	Department of Justice, Bureau of Justice Assistance
CAPPS II	Computer Assisted Passenger Prescreening System II
CCAD	Consolidated Crime and Analysis Database
CDT	Center for Democracy and Technology
DHS	Department of Homeland Security
DOJ	Department of Justice
FBI	Federal Bureau of Investigation
GAO	Government Accountability Office
HSIN	Homeland Security Information Network
IACP	International Association of Chiefs of Police
IRTPA	Intelligence Reform and Terrorism Prevention Act of 2004
IT	Information Technology
ISE	Information Sharing Environment
ISE SAR	Information Sharing Environment Suspicious Activity Report
ISE-SAR EE	Information Sharing Environment Suspicious Activity Report Evaluation Environment
JRSA	Joint Research and Statistics Association
JTTF	Joint Terrorism Task Force
LAPD	Los Angeles Police Department

LEOe	Law Enforcement Onlin
N-DEx	Law Enforcement National Data Exchange
NSI	Nationwide Suspicious Activity Report Initiative
ODNI	Office of the Director for National Intelligence
OMB	Office of Management and Budget
PM-ISE	Program Manager for the Information Sharing Environment
PMO	Program Management Office
RISS	Regional Information Sharing Systems Program
SAR	Suspicious Activity Report
SHSP	State Homeland Security Program
TIA	Total Information Awareness Program
UASI	Urban Area Security Initiative

End Notes

[1] National Commission on Terrorist Attacks Upon the United States, *The 9/11 Commission Report*, July 22, 2004, pp. 353-356 and 416-418, available at http://www.9-11 commission.gov. Hereafter: *9/11 Commission Report.*

[2] The Markle Task Force on National Security in the Information Age was convened to "recommend ways to improve national security decisions by transforming business processes and the way information is shared." The Task Force has published three reports: *Protecting America's Freedom in the Information Age*, October 2002; *Creating a Trusted Information Network for Homeland Security*, December 2003; *Mobilizing Information to Prevent Terrorism: Accelerating Development of a Trusted Information Sharing Environment*, July 2006. See Markle Foundation *Press Release*, March 10, 2009. These reports are available at http://www.markletaskforce.org/.

[3] Markle Task Force, *Protecting America's Freedom in the Information Age*, October 2002, p. 9. Hereafter: "Markle Report I."

[4] P.L. 108-458, Dec. 17, 2004, §1016(b), 118 STAT. 3665.

[5] Ibid.

[6] The latest report was submitted in June 2009 and is available at http://www.fas.org/irp/agency/ ise/2009report.pdf.

[7] John O. Brennan, Assistant to the President for Homeland Security and Counterterrorism, Memorandum to Cabinet Principals, "Strengthening Information Sharing and Access," July 2, 2009.

[8] For background on state and local fusion centers, see CRS Report RL34070, *Fusion Centers: Issues and Options for Congress*, by John Rollins.

[9] DHS, "National Network of Fusion Centers Fact Sheet," October 26, 2011, http://www.dhs.gov/ files/programs/gc_1296484657738.shtm. Hereafter: DHS, "National Network of Fusion Centers Fact Sheet."

[10] P.L. 110-53, Aug. 3, 2007, §511, 121 STAT. 322. Amends *Homeland Security Act of 2002* by adding §210A(j).

[11] DHS, "Fusion Center Locations and Contact Information," December 15, 2011, http://www. dhs.gov/files/programs/gc_1301685827335.shtm; U.S. Congress, Senate Homeland Security and Governmental Affairs Committee, *Eight Years After 9/11: Confronting the*

Terrorist Threat to the Homeland, Written Statement of Secretary of Homeland Security, Janet Napolitano, 111th Cong., 1st sess., September 30, 2009.

[12] DHS, "National Network of Fusion Centers Fact Sheet."

[13] Markle Task Force, "Nation At Risk: Policy Makers Need Better Information to Protect the Country," March 2009, p. 3.

[14] *Findings and Recommendations of the SAR Support and Implementation Project, Final Draft*, June 2008, p. 6. The SAR Support and Implementation Project was a joint effort of the Department of Justice (DOJ) Bureau of Justice Assistance; the Major Cities Chiefs Association, DOJ's Global Justice Information Sharing Initiative, the Criminal Intelligence Coordinating Council, and DHS to develop recommendations to be used by law enforcement agencies to improve identification and reporting of suspicious activity and the sharing of that information with fusion centers and Joint Terrorism Task Forces. See pp. 1-2.

[15] Ibid., p. 2.

[16] National Strategy for Information Sharing, October 2007, pp. 2-3.

[17] Markle Report I, p. 48.

[18] 9/11 Commission Report, p. 401.

[19] The Justice Research and Statistics Association (JRSA), *Information Sharing Systems: A Survey of Law Enforcement*, July 31, 2006, p. 6. For a list of these systems, see Appendix B of the survey. The JRSA, founded in 1974, is a national nonprofit organization of state Statistical Analysis Center directors, researchers, and practitioners throughout government, academia, and criminal justice organizations.

[20] Ibid., p. 4.

[21] The term "suspicious activity report" is used in many contexts to describe behavior or activity that may be associated with crime, terrorism included. Another example of the use of the term is in connection with the Department of the Treasury's requirement that certain financial institutions file reports of "any suspicious transaction relevant to a possible violation of law or regulation." 31 U.S.C., Section 1818(g)(1). The requirement to file reports of suspicious transactions applies to some financial institutions, including banks, thrifts, credit unions, insurance companies, casinos, mutual funds, futures commission merchants, securities brokers and dealers, and money services businesses.

[22] U.S. Congress, House Committee on Homeland Security, Subcommittee on Intelligence, Information Sharing, and Terrorism Risk Assessment, *Homeland Security Intelligence: Its Relevance and Limitations*, Statement of John W. Gaissert, Chief of Police; Commerce, Georgia, 111th Cong., 1st sess., March 18, 2009.

[23] Trooper Hanger had no reason to suspect a connection between McVeigh and the bombing in Oklahoma City. But the trooper's suspicions were raised when the driver looked at his bumper when told why he had been pulled over. Says Trooper Hanger: "I thought if he knew he didn't have a tag, why did he look at the back of the car like that? It just didn't seem right." In addition, McVeigh was unable to provide proof of insurance and a bill of sale for the vehicle and then disclosed that he had a firearm. Trooper Hanger arrested McVeigh for five misdemeanors and took him into custody. McVeigh was awaiting arraignment when the FBI connected him to the bombing. See National Law Enforcement Officers Memorial at http://www.nleomf.com/TheFund/programs/OOM/hanger_oct01.htm.

[24] U.S. Congress, House Committee on Homeland Security, Subcommittee on Intelligence, Information Sharing, and Terrorism Risk Assessment, *A Report Card on Homeland Security Information Sharing*, Statement of John McKay, Former U.S. Attorney for the Western District of Washington, 110th Cong., 2nd sess., September 24, 2008. Hereafter: McKay Testimony, September 24, 2008.

[25] DOJ Office of the Inspector General Special Report, "The FBI Laboratory: An Investigation into Laboratory Practices and Alleged Misconduct in Explosives-Related and Other Cases," Section H2, Yū Kikumura Factual Background, April 1997.

[26] James Jay Carafano, "U.S. Thwarts 19 Terrorist Attacks Against America Since 9/11," Heritage Foundation, Backgrounder #2085, November 13, 2007.

[27] St. Petersburg Times, "USF Terror Suspect Agrees to Plead Guilty," June 14, 2008, at http://tampabay.com/news/courts/criminal/article624049.ece.

[28] U.S. Congress, House Committee on Homeland Security, Subcommittee on Intelligence, Information Sharing, and Terrorism Risk Assessment, *Homeland Security Intelligence: Its Relevance and Limitations*, Statement of Joan T. McNamara, Assistant Commanding Officer, Counter Terrorism and Criminal Intelligence Bureau, Los Angeles Police Department, 111th Cong., 1st sess., March 18, 2009. Hereafter: McNamara Testimony, March 18, 2009.

[29] Ibid

[30] McKay Testimony, September 24, 2008.

[31] See *9/11 and Terrorist Travel, Staff Report of the National Commission on Terrorist Attacks on the United States,* August 21, 2004, p. 139. Atta, who piloted American Flight 11, the first plane to hit the World Trade Center, was stopped on April 26, 2001, near Tamarac, FL, and cited for driving without a license. After he failed to appear in court on this citation, a warrant was issued for his arrest. On July 5, 2001, a Delray Beach, Florida police officer stopped Atta for speeding but gave him only a warning. See "The Road to Ground Zero, Part Five: A Trail of Missed Opportunities," *The Sunday Times*, February 3, 2002, at http://s3.amazonaws.com/911timeline/2002/sundaytimes020302.html. Ziad Samir Jarrah, who was believed to have piloted United Flight 93 that crashed in Pennsylvania, was pulled over by Maryland state troopers two days before the attacks while speeding on Interstate 95. See CNN.com "Maryland Police Release Hijacker Traffic Stop Video," January 8, 2002, at http://archives.cnn.com/2002/US/01/08/inv.hijacker.video/index.html.

[32] NSI Project Overview Briefing by Russ Porter, Chairman of the Criminal Intelligence Coordinating Council of the Global Justice Information Sharing Initiative.

[33] National Strategy for Information Sharing, October 2007, p. 3.

[34] See Ibid., p. A1-6, and PM-ISE, *Fact Sheet: Nationwide Suspicious Activities Reporting Initiative*, December 23, 2008, p. 1, at http://www.ise.gov/docs/sar/Fact_Sheet_NSI_-_December_23_2008_Final.pdf.

[35] Ibid.

[36] *Nationwide SAR Initiative Annual Report, 2010,* http://nsi.ncirc.gov/documents/NSI_Annual_Report_2010_FINAL.pdf, p. 2. Hereafter: *Nationwide SAR Initiative Annual Report, 2010.*

[37] Ibid., p. 3.

[38] Federated search is the process of performing a simultaneous real-time search of multiple diverse and distributed sources from a single search page, with the federated search engine acting as intermediary. See Sol Lederman, "A Federated Search Primer, Part II," at http://www.altsearchengines.com/2009/01/12/a-federated-search-primer-part-ii-ofiii/

[39] Examples of this controversy can be found at Alice Lipowicz, "DHS' data mining sparks more controversy," *Federal Computer Week*, December 4, 2007, at http://fcw.com/articles/2007/12/04/dhs-data-mining-sparks-more-controversy.aspx; Susan Page, "NSA secret database report triggers fierce debate in Washington," *USA Today*, May 11, 2006, at http://www.usatoday.com/news/washington/2006-05-11-nsa-reax_x.htm; and William Safire, "You are a Suspect." *New York Times,* November 14, 2002, at http://www.nytimes.com/2002/11/14/opinion/you-are-a-suspect.html. See also Jeffrey A. Hart, "The Controversies over Data Mining and Warrantless Searches in the Wake of September 11," paper prepared for a panel on "Information Access, Power, and Rights," at the annual meeting of the International Studies Association, March 2008.

[40] PM-ISE, *Nationwide SAR Initiative Concept of Operations*, December 2008. p. 3, at http://www.ise.gov/docs/sar/NSI_CONOPS_Version_1_FINAL_2008-12-11_r5.pdf.

[41] These two steps involving review represent the two forms of vetting central to the SAR process. According to the PM-ISE, "Before an agency can move SARs from the agency systems to the ISE, two forms of vetting must occur. Supervisors who initially receive a

SAR from law enforcement officers, public safety agencies, private sector partners, or citizens must initially review the SAR to determine whether it has a nexus to terrorism and whether it includes the behaviors identified in the ISE-SAR Functional Standard. Trained analysts must then analyze the SAR against the behaviors identified in Part B of the ISE-SAR Functional Standard. Throughout the vetting process, privacy, civil rights, and civil liberties are vigilantly and actively protected through the training that analysts receive and through the system attributes that are a part of the NSI." See PM-ISE, *Privacy, Civil Rights, and Civil Liberties Analysis and Recommendations: Nationwide Suspicious Activity Reporting Initiative,* July 2010, p. 15, http://nsi.ncirc.gov/documents/NSI_PCRCL_Analysis_July_2010.pdf. Hereafter: PM-ISE, *Privacy, Civil Rights.*

[42] PM-ISE, *Information Sharing Environment (ISE), Functional Standard (FS) Suspicious Activity Reporting (SAR), Version 1.5,* May 21, 2009, pp. 7-11. http://www.dhs.gov/xlibrary/assets/privacy/privacy-pia-dhswide-sar-ise-appendix.pdf. Hereafter: PM-ISE, *ISE, FS, SAR Version 5.1.*

[43] McNamara Testimony, March 18, 2009.

[44] LAPD, "Terrorism Related Consolidated Crime and Analysis Database (CCAD) Codes," provided to CRS by the LAPD Counter-Terrorism and Criminal Intelligence Bureau, October 27, 2009.

[45] Mike German and Jay Stanley, American Civil Liberties Union, *Fusion Center Update*, July 2008, p. 2.

[46] U.S. Congress, House Committee on Homeland Security, Subcommittee on Intelligence, Information Sharing, and Terrorism Risk Assessment, *Homeland Security Intelligence: Its Relevance and Limitations*, Statement of Gregory T. Nojeim, Director on Freedom, Security, and Technology, Center for Democracy and Technology, 111th Cong., 1st sess., March 18, 2009. Hereafter: Nojeim Testimony, March 18, 2009.

[47] Nick Madigan, "Spying Uncovered," *Baltimore Sun*, July 18, 2008, at http://www.baltimoresun.com/news/local/bal-te.md.spy18jul18,0,3787307.story.

[48] Ibid.

[49] See "Guidelines to Ensure that the Information Privacy and Other Legal Rights of Americans are Protected in the Development and Use of the Information Sharing Environment," http://www.ise.gov/sites/default/files/PrivacyGuidelines20061204.pdf.

[50] *Nationwide SAR Initiative Annual Report, 2010,* p. 6.

[51] Ibid.

[52] PM ISE, *Fact Sheet: SAR Functional Standard in the ISE*, p. 3, at http://www.ise.gov/docs/ctiss/FactSheetCTISS_ISE-SAR.pdf.

[53] *2010 Nationwide SAR Initiative Annual Report,* p. 6.

[54] PM ISE, *Initial Privacy and Civil Liberties Analysis of the ISE-SAR Functional Standard and Evaluation Environment*, September 2008—Version 1. Hereafter: Initial Privacy and Civil Liberties Analysis of the ISE-SAR Functional Standard, September 2008, at http://www.ise.gov/docs/sar/ .ISE_SAR_Initial_Privacy_and_Civil_Liberties_Analysis.pdf

[55] Office of the PM-ISE briefing to CRS, July 20, 2009.

[56] PM-ISE, *Information Sharing Environment Functional Standard Suspicious Activity Reporting, Version 1.5*, May 21, 2009, at http://www.ncirc.gov/sar/ISE-FS-200_ISE-SAR_Functional_Standard_V1_5_Issued.pdf.

[57] PM-ISE, *ISE, FS, SAR Version 5.1;* Fact Sheet: Update to Suspicious Activity Reporting Functional Standard Provides Greater Privacy and Civil Liberties Protections, May 21, 2009, p. 1, at http://www.ise.gov/docs/ctiss/ISE-SAR_Functional_Standard_V1_5_Fact_Sheet.pdf.

[58] ACLU, Press Release, "Intelligence Community Raises Its Standards For Information Collection: Collaborative Effort Addresses Privacy and Civil Liberties Concerns," May 22, 2009, http://www.aclu.org/safefree/general/39656prs20090522.html.

[59] *2010 Nationwide SAR Initiative Annual Report,* p. 12.

[60] PM-ISE, *Privacy, Civil Rights,* p. 15.

[61] *2010 Nationwide SAR Initiative Annual Report,* pp. 7-9.
[62] See Robert Wasserman, *Guidance for Building Communities of Trust,* July 2010, pp. 4-5, http://nsi.ncirc.gov/documents/e071021293_BuildingCommTrust_v2-August%2016.pdf.
[63] Ibid.
[64] For more on the campaign see DHS, "'If You See Something, Say Something™' Campaign," December 12, 2011,http://www.dhs.gov/files/reportincidents/see-something-say-something.shtm.
[65] Ibid.
[66] *2010 Nationwide SAR Initiative Annual Report,* p. 14. See **Appendix A** for a description of *eGuardian*.
[67] *Suspicious Activity Reporting Process Implementation Checklist,* p. 16.
[68] Ibid. See **Appendix A** for a description of this system.
[69] See **Appendix A** for a description of the Guardian and *eGuardian* systems.
[70] Information about NSI information technology infrastructure requirements provided by Paul Wormeli, Executive Director of the IJIS institute.
[71] Ibid.
[72] NSI, "Training," http://nsi.ncirc.gov/training.aspx.
[73] Ibid.
[74] Ibid.
[75] Ibid.
[76] Secretary of DHS Janet Napolitano, "Remarks to The International Association of Chiefs of Police," October 25, 2011, http://www.dhs.gov/ynews/speeches/20111025-napolitano-remarks-iacp.shtm.
[77] *Nationwide SAR Initiative Annual Report, 2010,* p. 13.
[78] Office of the PM-ISE briefing to CRS, July 20, 2009.
[79] BJA, a component of DOJ's Office of Justice Programs, supports law enforcement, courts, corrections, treatment, victim services, technology, and prevention initiatives that strengthen the nation's criminal justice system. Among its activities, BJA provides technical advice and assistance to states and major urban areas on the development of their intelligence fusion centers. See DOJ *Global Justice Information Sharing Initiative*, 2009, p. 6.
[80] The Global Justice Information Sharing Initiative brings stakeholders together in five major working groups to collaborate on major information sharing challenges. The working groups are Global Infrastructure/Standards, Criminal Intelligence Coordinating Council, Global Intelligence, Global Privacy and Information Quality, and Global Security. See Ibid.
[81] Pilot sites are the Police Departments of Boston, Chicago, Houston, Las Vegas, Los Angeles, Miami-Dade, and Washington DC; Arizona Department of Public Safety (Arizona Counterterrorism Information Center); Florida Department of Law Enforcement; New York State Intelligence Center; Seattle Police Department/Washington State Fusion Center; and the Virginia Fusion Center.
[82] *Final Report: Information Sharing Environment (ISE)—Suspicious Activity Reporting (SAR) Evaluation Environment,* January 2010, http://nsi.ncirc.gov/documents/NSI_EE.pdf.
[83] Ibid., p. 5.
[84] Ibid., pp. 5-6.
[85] Ibid., p. 6
[86] NSI, "The Program Management Office," http://nsi.ncirc.gov/program_management_office.aspx.
[87] Ibid.
[88] Ibid.
[89] Nojeim Testimony, March 18, 2009.
[90] GAO, Homeland Security: Federal Efforts Are Helping to Alleviate Some Challenges Encountered by State and Local Information Fusion Centers, GAO-08-35, October 30, 2007.

[91] GAO, Interagency Collaboration: Key Issues for Congressional Oversight of National Security Strategies, Organizations, Workforce, and Information Sharing, GAO-09-904SP, September 2009, p. 50.

[92] Data was for the period July 2004 through November 2007. See DOJ, Office of the Inspector General Audit Division, *The FBI's Terrorist Threat and Suspicious Incident Tracking System,* Audit Report 09-02, November 2008, p. ii.

[93] Briefing to CRS by Thomas O'Reilly, DOJ Bureau of Justice Assistance, June 15, 2009.

[94] Markle Task Force on National Security in the Information Age, *Nation at Risk: Policy Makers Need Better Information to Protect the Country,* March 2009, p. 7.

[95] For details on the Global Federated Identity Management framework which provides a standards-based approach for implementing federated identity, see DOJ, Office of Justice Programs, Justice Information Sharing, "Security and Federated Identity Management" at http://www.it.ojp.gov/default.aspx?area=nationalInitiatives&page=1179.

[96] See FBI, "Law Enforcement Online" at http://www.fbi.gov/hq/cjisd/leo.htm.

[97] See DOJ, Office of Justice Programs, Bureau of Justice Assistance, "RISS Program Brief." http://www.riss.net/overview.aspx.

[98] See DHS, *HSIN*, February 10, 2009, at http://www.dhs.gov/xinfoshare/programs/gc_1156888108137.shtm.

[99] DOJ, "Law Enforcement Information Sharing Program (LEISP)," at http://www.usdoj.gov/jmd/ocio/leisp/.

[100] DOJ, "LEISP Initiatives," at http://www.usdoj.gov/jmd/ocio/leisp/initiatives.htm.

[101] FBI, "*eGuardian* Threat Tracking System," http://foia.fbi.gov/eguardian_threat.htm. Hereafter: "FBI, *eGuardian* Threat Tracking System."

[102] DOJ, Office of the Inspector General Audit Division, *The FBI's Terrorist Threat and Suspicious Incident Tracking System,* Audit Report 09-02, November 2008, p. 1.

[103] FBI, "Connecting the Dots: Using New FBI Technology," September 19, 2008, at http://www.fbi.gov/page2/sept08/eguardian_091908.html.

[104] FBI, "*eGuardian* Threat Tracking System."

In: Nationwide Suspicious Activity …
Editor: Laurits Hartmann

ISBN: 978-1-62618-766-5
© 2013 Nova Science Publishers, Inc.

Chapter 2

INFORMATION SHARING: ADDITIONAL ACTIONS COULD HELP ENSURE THAT EFFORTS TO SHARE TERRORISM-RELATED SUSPICIOUS ACTIVITY REPORTS ARE EFFECTIVE*

United States Government Accountability Office

WHY GAO DID THIS STUDY

In 2007, DOJ and its federal partners developed the Nationwide Suspicious Activity Reporting Initiative to establish a capability to gather and share terrorism-related suspicious activity reports. GAO was asked to examine the initiative's progress and performance. This report addresses the extent to which (1) federal agencies have made progress in implementing the initiative, and what challenges, if any, remain; (2) the technical means used to collect and share reports overlap or duplicate each other; (3) training has met objectives and been completed; and (4) federal agencies are assessing the initiative's performance and results. GAO analyzed relevant documents and interviewed federal officials responsible for implementing the initiative and stakeholders from seven states (chosen based on their geographic location and

* This is an edited, reformatted and augmented version of the Highlights of GAO-13-233, a report to congressional requesters, dated March 2013.

other factors). The interviews are not generalizable but provided insight on progress and challenges.

What GAO Recommends

GAO recommends that DOJ implement formalized mechanisms to provide stakeholders feedback on the suspicious activity reports they submit, mitigate risks from supporting two systems to collect and share reports that may result in the FBI not receiving needed information, more fully assess if training for line officers meets their needs, and establish plans and time frames for implementing measures that assess the homeland security results the initiative has achieved. DOJ agreed with these recommendations and identified actions taken or planned to implement them.

What GAO Found

The Department of Justice (DOJ) has largely implemented the Nationwide Suspicious Activity Reporting Initiative among fusion centers—entities that serve as the focal point within a state for sharing and analyzing suspicious activity reports and other threat information. The state and local law enforcement officials GAO interviewed generally said the initiative's processes worked well, but that they could benefit from additional feedback from the Federal Bureau of Investigation (FBI) on how the reports they submit are used. The FBI has a feedback mechanism, but not all stakeholders were aware of it. Implementing formalized feedback mechanisms as part of the initiative could help stakeholders conduct accurate analyses of terrorism-related information, among other things.

The technical means that federal, state, and local entities use to collect and share terrorism-related suspicious activity reports—Shared Spaces servers that DOJ provides to most fusion centers and the FBI's eGuardian system—provide many overlapping or duplicative services. For example, both systems provide a national network for sharing the reports and tools to analyze them. The federal government is aware that duplication exists but supports both systems to enable fusion centers to control information on individuals, consistent with the centers' privacy requirements, and facilitate the FBI's investigative needs. However, the FBI was concerned that supporting two systems introduces risks that it will not receive all reports. For example, at the time of our review, many fusion centers were choosing not to automatically share all of their reports with the FBI's system—although they may have shared reports via phone or other means—and DOJ had not fully diagnosed why. In its March 2013 letter commenting on a draft of this report, DOJ stated that it had made progress on this issue. DOJ also had not formally tested the exchange of information between the two systems to ensure that the exchanges were complete. Taking additional steps to mitigate the risks that reports are not fully shared could help DOJ ensure that the FBI receives all information that can support investigations.

Stakeholders GAO interviewed generally reported that training fully or partially met objectives, such as making law enforcement more aware of the initiative. DOJ has mechanisms to assess the analyst training to help ensure that analysts have the information they need to review and share reports. However, DOJ had not fully assessed its training provided to officers on the front line, which could help ensure that officers receive sufficient information to be able to recognize terrorism-related suspicious activity. DOJ has provided training to executives at 77 of 78 fusion centers, about 2,000 fusion center analysts, and about 290,000 of the 800,000 line officers. DOJ is behind schedule in training the line officers but is taking actions to provide training to officers who have not yet received it.

DOJ and other agencies collect some data to assess the performance of the Nationwide Suspicious Activity Reporting Initiative—such as the number of reports submitted and resulting FBI investigations. These data show that stakeholders were increasingly submitting and using terrorism-related reports. However, DOJ had not yet established plans and time frames for implementing measures that assess the homeland security results achieved by the initiative and thus lacked a means for establishing accountability for implementing them.

ABBREVIATIONS

ACS	Automated Case Support
DHS	Department of Homeland Security
DOD	Department of Defense
DOJ	Department of Justice
FBI	Federal Bureau of Investigation
I&A	Office of Intelligence and Analysis

ISA IPC	Information Sharing and Access Interagency Policy Committee
ISE	Information Sharing Environment
IT	information technology
JTTF	Joint Terrorism Task Force
NARA	National Archives Records Administration
NSI	Nationwide Suspicious Activity Reporting Initiative
PMO	NSI Program Management Office
PM-ISE	Program Manager for the Information Sharing Environment
SAR	Suspicious Activity Report

March 13, 2013

Congressional Requesters

The attempted car bombing of Times Square in May 2010 was a planned terrorist attack that was foiled when street vendors alerted a New York Police Department officer after they spotted smoke coming from a vehicle. Two days later, federal agents arrested a 30-year-old Pakistan- born resident of Connecticut who subsequently pleaded guilty for attempting to carry out the attack.

Every day, in the course of their duties, law enforcement officers at all levels of government—federal, state, local, and tribal—observe suspicious behaviors and receive information from concerned citizens, private security, and other government agencies, that could help detect, prevent, or deter a terrorist attack.

Consistent with provisions of law and executive branch policy addressing the need for information systems wherein state, local, and tribal law enforcement agencies could contribute potentially terrorism-related information, the federal government developed the Nationwide Suspicious Activity Reporting Initiative (NSI) in 2007.[1]

The NSI establishes a nationwide capability to gather and share Suspicious Activity Reports (SAR) that have a potential nexus to terrorism.[2] These reports facilitate the identification and mitigation of potential terrorist threats as well as analysis to determine whether there are emerging patterns or trends suggesting such threats. In March 2010, the Department of Justice (DOJ) established the NSI Program Management Office (PMO) to support nationwide implementation of standardized processes for sharing terrorism-related SARs among federal, state, and local law enforcement agencies.

To support NSI implementation, the PMO has facilitated the rollout of information-sharing technology and developed a training strategy designed to enhance law enforcement professionals' ability to identify, report, evaluate, and share terrorism-related SARs.

We have designated the sharing of terrorism-related information as high risk because of the significant challenges the federal government faces in sharing this information in a timely, accurate, and useful manner.[3] The NSI is a key government program intended to address such challenges. You requested that we assess the NSI's progress and performance. In response to your request, this report addresses the extent to which

- DOJ and other federal entities have made progress in implementing the NSI, and what challenges remain, if any;
- the technical means that NSI stakeholders use to collect and share SARs overlap or duplicate each other and any risks this overlap or duplication may introduce;
- NSI training has met objectives, the PMO has assessed the training, and the training has been completed; and
- the PMO has assessed how well the NSI is working and the homeland security results it has achieved.

To address these objectives, we analyzed NSI programmatic documents, such as the NSI concept of operations and annual reports, and analyzed DOJ data—including data on NSI implementation, training, costs, and results—from the inception of the PMO in fiscal year 2010 through fiscal year 2012. We also interviewed officials from the Program Manager for the Information Sharing Environment (PM-ISE), DOJ, and the Department of Homeland Security (DHS) who are responsible for overseeing NSI efforts.[4] We obtained information from DOJ officials who manage the data about the steps taken to ensure their accuracy, and found the data to be sufficiently reliable for the purposes of this report.

In addition, to address the first three objectives, we interviewed nonprobability samples of officials from entities participating in the NSI, including officials from seven state or major urban area fusion centers—entities that serve as the focal point within a state for sharing and analyzing threat information.[5]

We selected these centers based on their size, geographic location, and level of participation in the NSI, among other factors. At each center, we interviewed executives and analysts to obtain perspectives on NSI processes and related training they received. We also interviewed officials from each center who were familiar with their entities' systems for documenting and sharing terrorism-related SARs. Further, we interviewed Federal Bureau of Investigation (FBI) officials from field offices in proximity to the fusion centers we contacted who are responsible for investigating and analyzing SARs, as well as officials from five local law enforcement agencies in these locations who had taken NSI training.

To obtain perspectives from participating federal agencies, we interviewed officials from the Federal Protective Service and the Bureau of Alcohol, Tobacco, Firearms and Explosives, which we selected based upon these agencies having a large number of officers who have received NSI training. Although the views of the individuals in our samples provide valuable insight into the implementation of the NSI, they are not generalizable to all federal, state, and local entities participating in the NSI.

We took additional steps to address the second, third, and fourth objectives regarding NSI technology, training, and results, respectively. To address the second objective, we analyzed DOJ documentation regarding the two primary systems that stakeholders use to collect, share, and analyze SARs—the PMO's Shared Spaces and the FBI's eGuardian system—such as user manuals and implementation guides. We compared the services of each system to determine the extent to which they overlap or were duplicative and assessed the extent to which DOJ followed best practices for ensuring that the systems effectively exchange information.[6]

To address the third objective, we analyzed PMO documentation regarding training objectives, targets, and recipient feedback mechanisms using leading practices for training programs.[7] To address the fourth objective, we assessed the PMO's plans for measuring the results the NSI has achieved using best practices for program management.[8] Appendix I contains more details about our scope and methodology.

We conducted this performance audit from February 2012 to March 2013 in accordance with generally accepted government auditing standards. Those standards require that we plan and perform the audit to obtain sufficient, appropriate evidence to provide a reasonable basis for our findings and conclusions based on our audit objectives.

We believe that the evidence we obtained provides a reasonable basis for our findings and conclusions based on our audit objectives.

BACKGROUND

NSI Partners

The NSI is a federal initiative that involves a collaborative effort of a number of federal, state, local, and private sector partners. Their roles are described in table 1.

Nationwide SAR Process

The NSI builds upon established, but largely ad hoc, processes that law enforcement agencies have used for years to collect information on suspicious activities. In 2008, the PM-ISE—in coordination with the Executive Office of the President and state, local, and tribal partners— established a "Functional Standard" that defines processes for collecting and sharing SARs that have a potential nexus to terrorism. Among other things, the Functional Standard includes a set of behavior-based criteria for analysts to use to help them determine if a SAR has a potential nexus to terrorism—such as a breach or attempted intrusion, expressed or implied threat, or cyber attack—and should be shared with other NSI participants.[9] SARs that are determined to have a potential nexus to terrorism pursuant to the Functional Standard are known as ISE-SARs.[10]

The PMO, FBI, and other entities further clarified the business processes associated with sharing ISE-SARs in an April 2012 two-page bulletin. Figure 1 outlines the process for collecting, disseminating, and utilizing SARs.

Systems Used to Share ISE-SARs

The NSI leverages technologies—the ISE Shared Spaces and the FBI's eGuardian system—to facilitate the collection, dissemination, and utilization of ISE-SARs. Previously, federal, state, local, and tribal law enforcement entities generally stored SARs at the local agency level and used nonstandard methods—such as telephone, fax, or e-mail—to share SARs with the FBI. Law enforcement entities may continue to use these methods for submitting SARs to the FBI, but the development of Shared Spaces and eGuardian allows for electronic submission, sharing, and access to SARs for analysis nationwide.

Shared Spaces and eGuardian were created during the same time frame (2007 to 2009), and both systems were first implemented in 2008.

Table 1. Nationwide Suspicious Activity Reporting Initiative Partners

Partner	Role
Program Manager for the Information Sharing Environment (PM-ISE)	• Plan for, oversee implementation of, and manage the Information Sharing Environment (ISE)—an approach for sharing terrorism-related information that may include any method deemed necessary and appropriate— in accordance with the Intelligence Reform and Terrorism Prevention Act of 2004, as amended.[a] • Developed Suspicious Activity Report (SAR) processes that eventually became the Nationwide Suspicious Activity Reporting Initiative (NSI), spending approximately $8 million on SAR-related activities from fiscal years 2006 through 2009. • Transferred management of the NSI to the Department of Justice (DOJ) after the administration designated DOJ as the executive agent for the program in December 2009. • Issues government-wide guidelines and standards for the management and operations of the NSI, and the ISE more generally.
Program Management Office (PMO)	• Established within DOJ's Bureau of Justice Assistance in March 2010. • Responsible for implementing the NSI and assisting agencies with adopting compatible processes, policies, and standards that foster the sharing of SARs while ensuring that privacy, civil rights, and civil liberties are protected. • Developed training programs on identifying, reporting, evaluating, and sharing SARs to help prevent acts of terrorism. • Expended approximately $5.5 million in fiscal year 2010 and $4.1 million over fiscal years 2011 and 2012 to help implement the NSI.[b] Plans to spend up to an estimated $6.5 million in fiscal year 2013 to support NSI training and technology maintenance costs and enhancement, contingent upon available appropriations.
Federal Bureau of Investigation (FBI)	• Has jurisdiction over terrorism-related investigations and is responsible for investigating all terrorism-related SARs. • Established Joint Terrorism Task Forces (JTTF) to investigate terrorism-related activity in 103 cities nationwide, which include members from state and local law enforcement agencies as well as officials from other federal agencies, such as DHS and the Department of Defense (DOD). • Leads efforts to implement the NSI among federal entities. • Provides one of the technology platforms for the NSI (eGuardian), which is linked to the FBI's classified Guardian incident management system.
Department of Homeland Security (DHS)	• The Office of Intelligence and Analysis (I&A) is DHS's lead component with responsibilities for sharing terrorism-related information with all levels of government and the private sector. • I&A is responsible for implementing ISE initiatives at DHS, including the NSI, and coordinating DHS policy, training, and technical solutions related to the NSI. • I&A develops and distributes intelligence reports that are based in whole or in part on analysis of terrorism-related SARs shared through the NSI and provides training to fusion center personnel on SAR analysis methods and tools. DHS's Privacy Office and Office for Civil Rights and Civil Liberties also participate in NSI training.

Partner	Role
	• DHS's Office of Infrastructure Protection and I&A work together to implement the NSI among owners and operators of critical infrastructure—assets and systems vital to the economy or health of the nation—such as oil refineries, dams, and telecommunications.[c]
Information Sharing and Access Interagency Policy Committee	• Established in July 2009 within the Executive Office of the President to indentify information-sharing priorities, among other things. • Includes representation of participating ISE agencies—such as DOJ, DHS, and DOD—and provides oversight and guidance to the ISE. • Has a SAR Subcommittee that focuses on future high-level policies for federal SAR information sharing.
Fusion centers	• Focal points within states and localities for the receipt, analysis, gathering, and sharing of terrorism and other threat-related information, including SARs. • Generally owned and operated by state and local entities—with support from federal agencies—that collectively provide resources, expertise, and information to detect, prevent, and respond to criminal and terrorist activity. • Review SARs contributed by state and local entities within their jurisdictions—such as law enforcement agencies—to determine whether they are terrorism-related and should be shared through the NSI. • Analyze SARs and develop relevant products to disseminate to other NSI stakeholders to help identify and address immediate and emerging threats.
State, local, and tribal law enforcement and hometown security partners	• State, local, and tribal law enforcement agencies gather information regarding behaviors and incidents that may have a nexus to terrorism. The NSI creates a standardized process for collecting and sharing this information. • Hometown security partners—such as critical infrastructure owners and operators, firefighters, emergency medical service providers, and private sector security professionals—also have routine duties that position them to observe and report suspicious behaviors.

Source: GAO analysis of PM-ISE, DOJ, and DHS documents and interviews.

[a] See Pub. L. No. 108-458, § 1016, 118 Stat. 3638, 3664-70 (2004) (codified as amended at 6 U.S.C. § 485).

[b] Funding amounts do not include federal staff that support the PMO, which are provided by DOJ's Bureau of Justice Assistance, the FBI, DHS, and the PM-ISE. Staffing levels ranged from a total of 6.5 full-time equivalents in fiscal year 2010 to 4.75 full-time equivalents in fiscal year 2012. The $4.1 million expended in fiscal years 2011 and 2012 was from amounts appropriated in 2011.

[c] Consistent with Homeland Security Presidential Directive/HSPD-7 (Dec. 17, 2003), DHS has identified 18 critical infrastructure sectors: Food and Agriculture; Banking and Finance; Chemical; Commercial Facilities; Communications; Critical Manufacturing; Dams; Defense Industrial Base; Emergency Services; Energy; Government Facilities; Healthcare and Public Heath; Information Technology; National Monuments and Icons; Nuclear Reactors, Materials and Waste; Postal and Shipping; Transportation Systems; and Water. Presidential Policy Directive/PPD-21, issued February 12, 2013, revoked HSPD-7 and realigns the 18 sectors into 16 critical infrastructure sectors but also provides that plans developed pursuant to HSPD-7 shall remain in effect until specifically revoked or superseded.

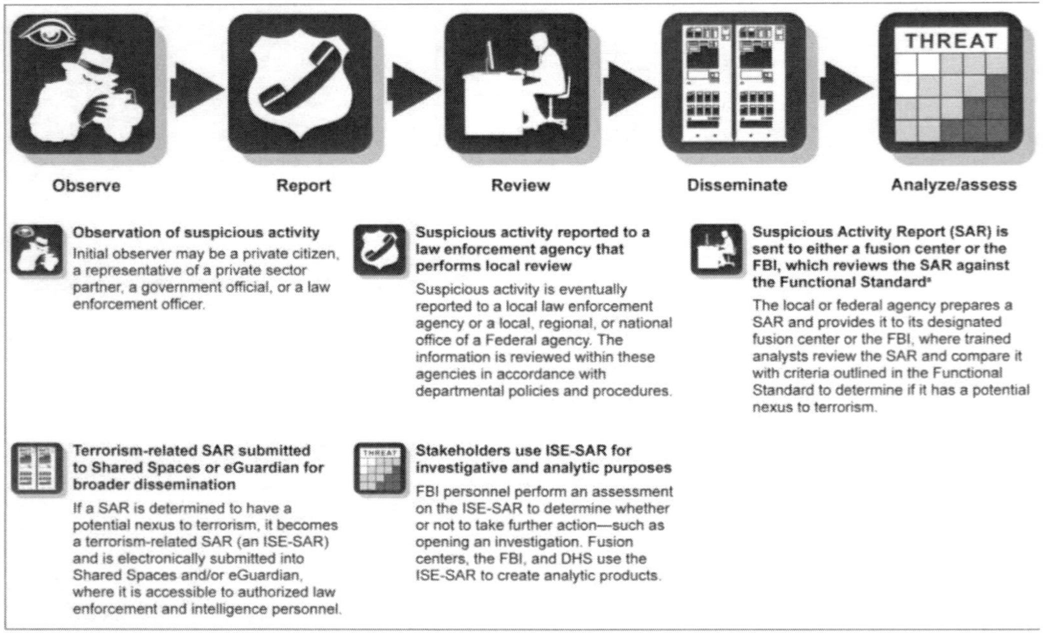

Source: GAO analysis of PM-ISE and DOJ documents; Art Explosion (clip art).

[a] According to FBI officials, the FBI uses the criteria in the eGuardian Privacy Impact Assessment (dated November 25, 2008) and the FBI's Domestic Investigations and Operations Guide to determine if SARs have a potential nexus to terrorism. The officials said that these criteria are generally consistent with the Functional Standard and the FBI and PMO are taking steps to further harmonize the criteria.

Figure 1. Nationwide Process for Collecting, Disseminating, and Utilizing Terrorism-related Suspicious Activity Reports.

The PMO has provided Shared Spaces servers to most fusion centers across the country. These servers allow centers to store ISE-SARs locally and retain ownership and exclusive control over modifying and deleting them, consistent with state laws and regulations and fusion center policies designed to protect privacy.[11] ISE-SARs that are modified or deleted in a fusion center's information system are subsequently modified or deleted in its Shared Spaces server through a regularly scheduled update process. A search tool called the NSI Federated Search allows fusion centers to use a single query to view ISE-SARs located on Shared Spaces servers across the country.

The FBI's eGuardian system is an unclassified part of the FBI's secret-level counterterrorism incident management system (Guardian) that is used to support the FBI's investigative needs. eGuardian was created to bridge the gap between the classified Guardian system and the sensitive but unclassified law enforcement environment. eGuardian's Privacy Impact Assessment notes that all SARs submitted to eGuardian remain the property and under the control of the submitting agency. All ISE-SARs that fusion centers submit to eGuardian are forwarded to Guardian.[12] The FBI may also send unclassified information from Guardian to eGuardian. eGuardian has a search tool that allows users to view eGuardian ISE- SARs submitted by users nationwide. To make ISE-SARs in eGuardian searchable and viewable to Federated Search users, the FBI maintains an eGuardian Shared Spaces server and forwards all eGuardian ISE- SARs to this server.[13]

Privacy and Civil Liberties

Federal, state, and local agencies have taken steps to help address the protection of privacy, civil rights, and civil liberties during the nationwide SAR process. For example, the NSI definition of a SAR was developed with input from several privacy, civil rights, and civil liberties advocacy groups. In addition, the Functional Standard uses behavior-based criteria for determining whether an activity has a potential nexus to terrorism— such as attempting to enter a restricted area or protected site—and notes that SARs should not be based solely on First Amendment-protected activities or factors, such as race, ethnicity, or religion. The Functional Standard also defines "personal information" as any information that may be used to identify individuals, such as an address, Social Security number, or license plate, and identifies which data elements within SARs may contain such personal information. The Functional Standard further recognizes that laws that prohibit or otherwise limit the sharing of personal information vary considerably among federal, state, local, and tribal levels.

To facilitate lawful information sharing, the technical means for sharing information nationwide—Shared Spaces and eGuardian—both have capabilities that enable agencies to safeguard personal information. Furthermore, the NSI developed a Privacy Framework that fusion centers and federal agencies who share ISE-SARs through the NSI must adopt prior to participating. Specifically, the framework requires that participating entities (1) have an approved privacy policy in place that meets minimum requirements, such as ensuring data quality and security, prior to sharing ISE-SARs through the NSI; (2) use the Functional Standard to vet and determine if SARs have a potential nexus to terrorism; and (3) incorporate the delivery of privacy training.

DHS has also supported fusion centers in their self-initiated efforts to perform peer-to-peer audits to help ensure their continued adherence to SAR privacy protections, among other things.

According to DHS officials, as of December 2012, fusion centers had completed 20 peer-to-peer privacy audits. The officials noted that some centers choose to conduct their own internal reviews or they are conducted by their parent agencies. In fiscal year 2013, the PMO plans to introduce a self-audit process for fusion centers to review their submission of ISE-SARs to ensure they adhere to the Functional Standard.

ALMOST ALL FUSION CENTERS AND 53 FEDERAL AGENCIES ARE PARTICIPATING IN THE NSI, BUT FEEDBACK ON THE USE OF SARS COULD BE ENHANCED

Most fusion centers and federal law enforcement agencies can now share ISE-SARs through the NSI. Participants we interviewed generally said that the NSI process is working well, but some state and local officials said that additional feedback on how the SARs are used could help them better contribute to the NSI.

FBI officials we interviewed were concerned that fusion center processes for reviewing SARs may prevent them from receiving all SARs in a timely manner. The PMO and FBI are taking steps to revise NSI guidance to address the FBI's concerns.

NSI Stakeholders Have Established the Capability to Share ISE-SARs at 74 of 78 Fusion Centers and 53 Federal Agencies

The PMO has largely implemented the NSI at fusion centers, which in turn allows all law enforcement agencies within the fusion centers' jurisdictions to begin providing ISE-SARs as part of the NSI. The PMO and DHS have also begun training other homeland security partners— such as critical infrastructure owners and operators and emergency medical technicians—to identify and report terrorism-related SARs to the NSI. FBI officials said they have reached out to all federal departments and are implementing the NSI at agencies that have law enforcement or military force protection personnel that would be in a position to observe suspicious activity.[14] The officials said they are determining if there are any additional agencies that should participate. Table 2 contains additional information on NSI implementation.

Selected State and Local Participants Reported the SAR Process Generally Worked Well, but More Feedback on the Use of SARs Could Help them Improve Reporting

Officials from 6 of the 7 fusion centers and 4 of the 5 local law enforcement agencies we interviewed said that the NSI process for vetting and submitting potentially terrorism-related SARs generally worked well for them.[15] The officials cited a number of benefits from their participation in the NSI. For example, they reported that

- having the ability to view ISE-SARs from across the nation has allowed their fusion center to conduct analysis to identify trends of concern and potential threats,
- an increase in the quality of ISE-SARs has led to better information on potential terrorist threats,
- the Functional Standard has led to a common understanding of what terrorism-related ISE-SARs are and has helped protect privacy and civil liberties when sharing ISE-SARs, and
- officers have a better understanding of suspicious activities that may be indicative of terrorism and the importance of reporting SARs.

Table 2. Nationwide Suspicious Activity Reporting Initiative Implementation

Entity type	Participation requirements	Participation status
Fusion centers	Technical requirements for sharing and analyzing Suspicious Activity Reports (SAR): • obtain access to eGuardian (obtaining a Shared Spaces server is optional); and • obtain access to the NSI Federated Search tool. Policy requirements to protect privacy, civil rights, and civil liberties: • enter into a participation agreement with the Nationwide Suspicious Activity Reporting Initiative (NSI) Program Management Office (PMO); • have at least one analyst trained to vet against the Functional Standard, enter into eGuardian or Shared Spaces, and analyze SARs; • have an approved privacy policy in place; and • have an approved site plan that describes the center's procedures and technology for implementing the SAR process.	According to PMO officials, as of February 2013, 74 of 78 fusion centers had established the capability to share SARs: • 72 of 78 fusion centers had implemented all technical and policy requirements (54 fusion centers also had a Shared Spaces server); • 2 fusion centers had implemented the technical requirements required to share SARs but had not completed the policy requirements; • 2 fusion centers intended to participate in the NSI but had not yet completed the technical or policy requirements; and • 2 fusion centers had opted to not participate in the NSI;[a]
State, local, and tribal law enforcement	No requirements are set for state, local, and tribal law enforcement agencies to participate in the NSI.	According to PMO data, as of November 2012, more than 14,200 local law enforcement agencies in 46 states; Washington, D.C.; and 2 U.S. territories had the capability to share ISE-SARs through the 74 fusion centers where the NSI is being implemented.

Entity type	Participation requirements	Participation status
Hometown security partners	No specific requirements are set for hometown security partners to be able to report SARs. The PMO and DHS are working with key critical infrastructure and public safety associations to launch an outreach campaign to help provide training to hometown security partners.	• As of February 2013, more than 52,800 hometown security partners had received training. • As of May 2012, 6 of 18 DHS-recognized critical infrastructure sectors were able to submit SAR data through DHS's Homeland Security Information Network, a secure web- based portal for information sharing. • PMO officials said they plan to introduce maritime sector–focused SAR training in fiscal year 2013.
Federal agencies	Technical and policy requirements to participate in the NSI: • obtain access to eGuardian, • receive an executive-level briefing, • enter into a participation agreement with the PMO to document participation in the NSI, • establish a SAR protocol that describes the process for reviewing and submitting SARs, adhere to a privacy policy, and • complete training for frontline officers and analysts. Federal agencies have the option of obtaining a Shared Spaces server.	According to the FBI, as of November 2012: • 27 federal agencies and the Department of Defense had met all technical and policy requirements; and • 26 federal agencies had met all requirements except for completing analyst training.[b] • DHS and the Department of Transportation had decided to obtain Shared Spaces servers. All other federal agencies are using eGuardian as their means of sharing SARs.

Source: GAO analysis of DOJ documents and interviews with DOJ officials.

[a] PMO officials said these fusion centers opted not to participate in the NSI and therefore do not enter SARs into Shared Spaces or eGuardian because of state legal restrictions on sharing SARs in this manner.

[b] Appendix III provides a list of the 53 federal agencies participating in the NSI.

These views were consistent with national law enforcement organizations' views—such as those of the International Association of Chiefs of Police and the Major Cities Chiefs Association—which have supported the creation of the NSI and its implementation nationwide.

Fusion center and local law enforcement agency officials we interviewed generally said that receiving additional feedback on the SARs they submit—such as whether the FBI has received the SARs, whether the FBI is investigating the SARs, or what the outcomes of any investigations are—would help them better contribute to the NSI. Specifically, executives from all 7 of the fusion centers, analysts from 6 of the 7 fusion centers, and officials from all 5 local law enforcement agencies we interviewed said that receiving feedback on the outcome of SARs they submit was important. They noted, for instance, that feedback reinforces that there is value in reporting, helps to identify what threats exist in their area so that they know what to look for, helps to ensure their SARs are accurate, and encourages officers to continue reporting.[16]

The FBI has established a mechanism to provide feedback on ISE-SARs through eGuardian, but not all of the stakeholders we interviewed were aware of or had access to this mechanism. Specifically, the FBI uses eGuardian to inform stakeholders of whether it has determined through an initial assessment if the ISE-SAR has (1) a potential nexus to terrorism and warrants an investigation, (2) an inconclusive nexus to terrorism, or (3) no nexus to terrorism. FBI officials noted that eGuardian also provides the SAR submitter details about when the SAR was received by the FBI; which FBI field office is investigating the SAR; and contact information if the fusion center or state, local, or tribal law enforcement officials want additional information about the SAR. However, not all stakeholders use eGuardian and thus would not see this feedback. For example, while all fusion centers participating in the NSI have access to eGuardian, they may choose to use the Federated Search tool rather than eGuardian to review ISE-SARs and conduct analysis. Local law enforcement agencies are eligible to receive eGuardian accounts, but they do not need one to participate in the NSI, as they can provide SAR information to fusion centers or the FBI through other means, such as phone calls or e-mails. Officials from 3 of the 7 fusion centers we interviewed said they did not use eGuardian to review ISE-SAR data and officials from 2 of the 5 law enforcement agencies we interviewed said they did not have an eGuardian account. Moreover, executives and analysts from 4 of the 7 fusion centers we interviewed were not aware that this feedback existed.

To help ensure that NSI participants receive feedback, the PM-ISE recommended in February 2010 that the PMO formalize NSI feedback mechanisms, but the PMO has not yet done so. Specifically, formalized feedback mechanisms were to ensure that at a minimum (1) organizations that receive SARs—such as fusion centers and the FBI— notify entities that submit SARs when information they provide is designated as a ISE-SAR and shared, and (2) fusion center or FBI personnel notify all NSI participants when further evidence leads them to determine that a ISE-SAR should no longer be designated as being terrorism-related so that the original information does not continue to be used as the basis for analysis or action.[17] Discontinuing use of such SARs, when applicable, may also address concerns related to the protection of privacy and civil liberties. According to PMO officials, formalized feedback mechanisms have not been established because they thought it would be best to let each fusion center determine if and how to elicit and provide feedback. However, as our work indicated, most of the fusion center officials we interviewed had not established such mechanisms and were not aware that the FBI provided feedback.

Standards for Internal Control in the Federal Government notes that management should ensure there are adequate means of communicating with, and obtaining information from, external stakeholders that may have a significant impact on achieving program objectives.[18] Implementing formalized NSI feedback mechanisms—which could include leveraging existing mechanisms such as those in eGuardian—and communicating these mechanisms to stakeholders could help ensure that NSI stakeholders receive the information they need to enforce SAR policies designed to protect privacy considerations, maintain situational awareness, conduct accurate analyses, or motivate personnel to continue to report SARs.

Selected Federal Participants Reported the NSI Process Generally Worked Well; Agencies Are Addressing FBI Concerns about Potentially Not Receiving Some Information

Officials from five of the seven JTTFs we interviewed, the Federal Protective Service, and the Bureau of Alcohol, Tobacco, Firearms and Explosives said that the NSI process to vet and submit SARs generally worked well for them.[19] For example, officials from four of the JTTFs said that the process had helped them receive more SARs from state and local agencies.

Further, none of the JTTF officials believed that the NSI process had led to an overload of nonrelevant information. Officials from the Federal Protective Service and the Bureau of Alcohol, Tobacco, Firearms and Explosives said that the NSI has contributed to an increase in the number of ISE-SARs they submit.

However, FBI officials from headquarters and all seven JTTFs we interviewed said that they had concerns that the FBI may not be receiving all available terrorism-related information because some fusion centers may share only ISE-SARs with the FBI—that is, SARs that have been determined to have a potential nexus to terrorism consistent with the Functional Standard criteria. They explained that the Functional Standard criteria are not as broad as the FBI's guidelines for investigating terrorism-related information.[20] For example, FBI headquarters officials said that certain terrorism-related activities—such as those related to terrorist financing, known terrorism subject location, and past terrorism event information—currently are not among the behavior-based criteria in the Functional Standard but would meet the FBI's guidelines. FBI officials did not have readily available data on the extent to which SARs that do not meet the Functional Standard criteria are provided to the FBI. Officials from four of the JTTFs we interviewed said that they had coordinated with the fusion centers in their jurisdictions to inform the fusion centers that they should provide all potentially terrorism-related information and not just ISE-SARs that met the Functional Standard. Officials from one JTTF noted that the state's fusion center had provided approximately 270 suspicious incident reports containing potentially terrorism-related information from June 2011 to October 2012, but only about 10 percent of them met the Functional Standard and were entered into Shared Spaces by the fusion center.

The extent to which the fusion center officials we interviewed said they provide SARs that did not meet the Functional Standard to the FBI varied. Officials from 3 fusion centers said that they would always or most of the time provide SARs that did not meet the Functional Standard to the FBI; officials from 3 fusion centers said they would provide these SARs some of the time or occasionally based on their professional judgment; and officials from 1 fusion center said that they would never provide these SARs to the FBI, in accordance with the fusion center's privacy policy. PMO and FBI officials said that they were working together to address this issue and develop a new version of the Functional Standard that is intended to harmonize the criteria that the FBI and fusion centers use to share ISE-SARs within the NSI. PMO officials said that the new Functional Standard will also provide guidance on sharing SARs with the FBI that do not meet the Functional Standard to help ensure that the FBI receives all relevant terrorism-related information while still protecting privacy and civil liberties. As of November 2012, PMO officials said that the draft of the new Functional Standard was completed and was awaiting PM-ISE and Information Sharing and Access Interagency Policy Committee (ISA IPC) review and approval. In the meantime, PMO officials said that when fusion center personnel contact them with questions about whether or not to share a SAR, the officials advise the personnel to share the information with the FBI.

Officials from FBI headquarters and four JTTFs we interviewed also had concerns that fusion centers may be taking steps to investigate SARs— such as interviewing the individuals engaged in suspicious activity or who witnessed suspicious activity—before providing the SARs to the FBI.[21]

Officials from 3 of the 7 fusion centers we interviewed said that they may do investigative work as part of their vetting process.[22] An official from one of these fusion centers explained that conducting some preliminary investigative work as part of the vetting process allows the center to better determine if the incident should be reported as an ISE-SAR. However, according to FBI officials, by conducting independent investigative work, fusion centers could disrupt ongoing FBI investigations or inappropriately dismiss a SAR and not provide relevant terrorism- related information to the FBI. PMO officials said that they have limited ability to control investigative procedures at state and local agencies, but the PMO's analytical training materials note that the vetting process should not include investigating. Further, PMO officials said that they plan to make a training video available in March 2013 that will further clarify that investigative work is not an appropriate part of vetting procedure.

Maintaining Two Systems That Duplicate the Function of Sharing ISE-SARs Introduces Risks That Have Not Been Fully Addressed

The NSI leverages the ISE Shared Spaces and the FBI's eGuardian system to collect and share ISE-SARs. The two systems have overlapping goals and offer duplicative services, but also have some unique features The federal government has decided to support both systems to meet users' differing needs. However, maintaining two systems introduces the risk that the FBI may not be able to review all potential terrorist threats because many fusion centers have decided not to automatically share all of their ISE-SARs with eGuardian, and the interconnection between the systems has not been fully tested. The PMO and FBI have taken steps to mitigate these risks, but they have not been fully addressed.

Shared Spaces and eGuardian Both Serve Fusion Centers and Provide Many Duplicative Services

As of November 2012, a total of 74 fusion centers had the capability to share ISE-SARs, of which 54 centers had a Shared Spaces server and all 74 centers had eGuardian accounts.[23] In general, fusion centers use Shared Spaces servers to store ISE-SAR information locally and authorize other fusion centers to view their ISE-SARs, and use eGuardian to share ISE-SARs with the FBI and other eGuardian users. Fusion centers have the option to submit ISE-SARs to Shared Spaces only, to eGuardian only, or to both Shared Spaces and eGuardian. According to PMO officials, fusion centers that submit ISE-SARs only to Shared Spaces provide them to the FBI through other means—such as telephone, e-mail, or fax. ISE-SARs that users submit only to eGuardian are forwarded to the FBI's Shared Spaces server, where they are accessible to users of Shared Spaces. Fusion centers provided different reasons for choosing to use one or both systems. For example, officials at 1 fusion center said they chose to use Shared Spaces because, among other things, it offered them the ability to remove ISE-SARs at their discretion—meaning that once they remove an ISE-SAR from their server, it may no longer be viewed by another party through the Federated Search—which is required for them to comply with their fusion center's privacy policy. Officials at another center said they chose eGuardian because FBI officials visited them and explained the system before they were made aware of Shared Spaces.

We have previously reported that overlap occurs when programs have similar goals, devise similar strategies and activities to achieve those goals, or target similar users; and duplication occurs when two or more agencies or programs are engaged in the same activities or provide the same services to the same beneficiaries. Since their creation, both Shared Spaces and eGuardian have provided many of the same services, including a nationwide network for sharing ISE-SARs and capabilities to analyze them for patterns and trends. Shared Spaces and eGuardian also contain much of the same information. Figure 2 shows the services that both Shared Spaces and eGuardian provide, as well as services that are unique to each system.

See Tables 4 and 5 in Appendix IV for additional information.

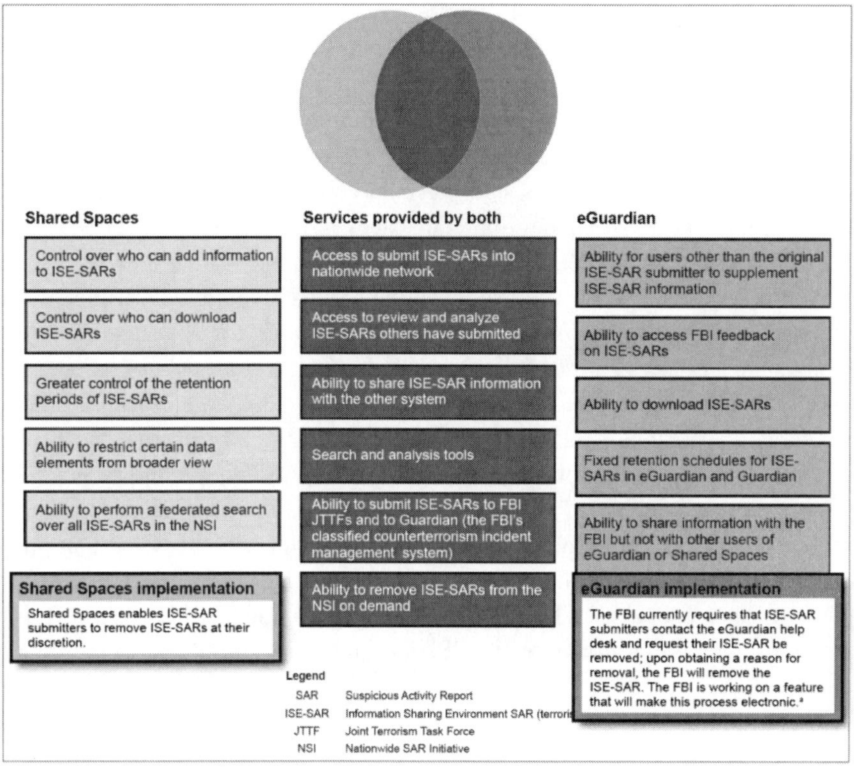

Source: GAO analysis of DOJ documents and interviews.

[a] In commenting on a draft of this report, FBI officials noted that in February 2013, the FBI implemented a new feature in eGuardian that allows fusion centers to directly and electronically remove their ISE-SARs.

Figure 2. Similar and Unique Services Provided by Shared Spaces and eGuardian.

According to PM-ISE officials, Shared Spaces was created in part based on fusion centers' feedback indicating that having control over the ISE- SARs they submit was essential for complying with state and local laws, regulations, and policies that are intended to protect the privacy rights of individuals in their jurisdiction. The officials added that eGuardian was not sufficient for providing that control. For example, the officials explained that they received feedback from fusion centers that the FBI process of automatically uploading ISE-SARs from eGuardian into the FBI's classified Guardian system limits fusion centers' control over their submitted ISE-SAR information. PMO officials also noted the importance of the "read-only" nature of Shared Spaces as a significant privacy protection. They explained that ISE-SAR contributors have proprietary rights over their information and expose it to others only upon the basis of another's query for viewing purposes—downloading, deleting, or otherwise modifying information in Shared Spaces is not possible. DHS officials added that this read-only feature safeguards against amassing copies of datasets that may be inaccurate or out of date.

As a result, PMO officials said that Shared Spaces and eGuardian should both continue to exist since Shared Spaces provides fusion centers with exclusive control over the ISE-SARs they submit and eGuardian serves the FBI's investigative needs. The officials noted that state and local leaders have endorsed the Shared Spaces model as the framework for sharing ISE-SARs among state and local entities.

FBI officials recognized that some fusion centers may prefer to use Shared Spaces as their primary means of sharing ISE-SARs and said that the FBI is satisfied with this arrangement as long as ISE-SARs in Shared Spaces are automatically shared with eGuardian.[24] However, in the FBI's opinion, it would not be cost effective for fusion centers—for which eGuardian fully meets their ISE-SAR sharing needs and is a center's preferred approach—to switch to Shared Spaces. The FBI noted that approximately half of the fusion centers use eGuardian to share ISE- SARs, and do so at no cost to the fusion centers.

Determining whether the federal government was investing significant resources in maintaining both systems proved difficult. The FBI provided costs for the overall Guardian system, but it did not separate the costs for the eGuardian component.[25] According to PMO officials, federal costs for the development, operations, and maintenance of Shared Spaces totaled about $600,000 from fiscal year 2010 through fiscal year 2012, and are expected to total about $1.26 million for fiscal years 2013 through 2015. The PMO did not know the costs that fusion centers and other owners of Shared Spaces servers bear, but had heard anecdotally that these costs were not significant. Although the PMO initially provided Shared Spaces servers to fusion centers, PMO officials said that the federal government does not plan to pay any replacement costs for them and that given the expected 7-year useful life of the servers, any cost estimate would be speculative. The officials noted that state and local entities would pay any replacement costs.

The PM-ISE is aware that Shared Spaces and eGuardian duplicate many services but said that both systems are currently needed to meet users' differing needs.[26] The PM-ISE noted that representatives from the PM- ISE, DOJ, DHS, FBI, and Office of the Director of National Intelligence who serve on the ISA IPC have participated in efforts that formally recognize the two-system approach, such as the unified message to NSI stakeholders that we discuss later in this report. We have similarly reported that in some instances of overlap or duplication, it may be appropriate for multiple agencies or entities to be involved in the same programmatic or policy area because of the nature or magnitude of the federal effort, and that many of the meaningful results that the federal government seeks to achieve require the coordinated efforts of more than one federal agency and often more than one sector and level of government.

Maintaining Both Shared Spaces and eGuardian Introduces Risks, Which Have Not Been Fully Addressed

Twenty-six Fusion Centers Were Not Always Simultaneously Submitting ISE- SARs to Shared Spaces and eGuardian

The FBI expressed concern that fusion centers were not always simultaneously submitting ISE-SARs to eGuardian when they submitted them to Shared Spaces, and DOJ was not fully aware of the reasons why. According to a November 2011 document, DOJ's Bureau of Justice Assistance and the FBI believed there were upwards of 1,000 ISE-SARs that were in Shared Spaces but not eGuardian.[27] The document noted that that this was an unacceptable risk to the country because the FBI needs to receive what may be time-sensitive information to ensure ISE- SARs can be tracked and accountability processes are in place for analysis and investigative purposes. According to FBI officials, by November 2012, the FBI and fusion centers had subsequently accounted for 700 to 800 of the 1,000 ISE-SARs, but could not confirm that the remaining 200 to 300 ISE-SARs were provided to the FBI.

To address the FBI's concern, in November 2011, the Deputy Attorney General issued a memo to fusion center directors that was intended to ensure that all fusion centers that had a Shared Spaces server implement an electronic capability to simultaneously submit ISE-SARs to both Shared Spaces and eGuardian. The memo noted that the FBI has the lead responsibility for investigating terrorism threats and eGuardian is the only federal system designed to accept and track leads for counterterrorism investigations. In December 2011, the Associate Attorney General and the Deputy Director of the FBI sent a memo to the Deputy Attorney General that outlined steps the PMO and FBI would take to ensure that terrorism-related information collected within the NSI is reported to the FBI through eGuardian, which included the following:[28]

- A 90-day period wherein if a user chose to submit an ISE-SAR to Shared Spaces but not eGuardian, the user was to provide an explanation as to why that user chose to do so.
- During this period, the PMO was to conduct weekly audits to determine which fusion centers were not sharing ISE-SARs with eGuardian and their reasons why. The PMO and FBI would then follow up with those centers to identify the nature of the issues (e.g., technical, legal, or policy-based) and the best way to address them.
- After this period, fusion centers were to no longer have the option to withhold ISE-SARs from eGuardian that they submit to Shared Spaces.

PMO and FBI officials subsequently reached out to fusion centers regarding this issue—which included conference calls and formal correspondence—but the steps outlined above were not fully implemented.[29] The Director of the PMO explained that fusion centers own and operate Shared Spaces servers, and the PMO cannot compel them to share ISE-SARs with eGuardian. The director noted, however, that when fusion centers do not share SARs with eGuardian, they have other means to provide them to the FBI—such as e-mail or telephone. PMO officials added that some centers cited privacy concerns as the reason for not sharing with eGuardian, but they did not know the specific reasons why many fusion centers were not sharing at the time of our review. In its March 2013 letter commenting on a draft of this report, DOJ stated that it had made progress on this issue.[30]

Before this update on its progress, PMO officials stated that a total of 74 fusion centers had the capability to collect and share ISE-SARs, of which:

- Twenty-eight centers submitted ISE-SARs to both Shared Spaces and eGuardian in all cases.
- Twenty-three centers submitted ISE-SARs to Shared Spaces in all cases and to eGuardian on a case-by-case basis. Fusion centers that do not submit ISE-SARs to eGuardian can provide them to the FBI through other means—such as telephone, fax, or email.
- Three centers were using Shared Spaces only to collect and share ISE-SARs and did not submit them to eGuardian. Executives and analysts from these centers said that they were concerned about their ability to remove ISE-SARs from eGuardian, which would be needed to be consistent with the fusion centers' privacy policies.[31] They noted that

their fusion centers always provide ISE-SARs to the FBI, and do so through telephone or other means.

- Twenty centers were using eGuardian only to collect and share ISE-SARs and did not submit them directly into Shared Spaces, although ISE-SARs in eGuardian are forwarded to the FBI's Shared Spaces server and made available to users of Shared Spaces.

To help make fusion centers more comfortable with automatically providing ISE-SARs to eGuardian, the FBI has taken actions to provide users with additional controls over the ISE-SARs they submit to eGuardian. For example, the privacy policies at two fusion centers we contacted require ISE-SARs to be removed from systems when the information has no further value or meets criteria for removal. This differed from eGuardian's policy that, according to FBI officials, allowed for ISE-SARs that are found to have no nexus to terrorism to remain in eGuardian for 180 days.[32] Officials at 1 of these centers said that they were also concerned about the differing retention periods of ISE-SARs in Guardian and other FBI systems.[33] In response to similar concerns from a number of fusion centers, the FBI modified the retention period in Guardian to more closely mirror the 5-year retention period in eGuardian and Shared Spaces, which the FBI believes addresses all fusion center concerns about retaining ISE-SARs.[34] Further, the FBI has created a feature within eGuardian that allows users to electronically submit SARs to the FBI without having them viewable to other users of eGuardian and Shared Spaces, which FBI officials said should address concerns about sharing personal information broadly.

The FBI's actions, implemented and planned, may address some of the concerns that fusion centers raised to us, but many centers still were not sharing all of their ISE-SARs with eGuardian at the time of our review. In addition, FBI officials noted that relying on telephone, fax, or e-mail versus automated means to share ISE-SARs introduces the risk that the FBI will not receive them. In our draft report that we provided to DOJ for comment, we noted that by reaching out to individual fusion centers to identify and address their specific concerns about entering ISE-SARs into eGuardian, the PMO and FBI could help ensure that the FBI will receive all ISE-SARs in a timely manner. In addition, establishing time frames to carry out these plans could improve accountability, as the PMO and FBI have previously committed to take similar steps but did not fully carry them out.

In its March 2013 letter commenting on a draft of this report, DOJ stated that since January 2013, an additional 21 fusion centers had begun to automatically share ISE-SARs with eGuardian. DOJ noted that of the remaining 7 fusion centers that were not automatically sharing ISE-SARs with eGuardian, 3 centers were submitting them electronically to eGuardian through other means, 1 center had temporarily suspended automatic submissions until a technical issue was corrected on their local server, 1 center had recently agreed to implement automatic sharing and was in the process of doing so, and 2 centers had identified legal issues that prevented them from adopting the automatic sharing solution. DOJ stated that PMO and FBI officials were involved in ongoing discussions with the leadership of the 2 fusion centers that raised legal concerns to identify what steps could be taken to mitigate those concerns.

Automated Exchanges of ISE- SARs between Systems Have Not Been Fully Tested

The PMO and FBI have modified the technical capabilities of Shared Spaces and eGuardian to enable electronic exchanges of ISE-SARs between systems, but the entities have not tested the data exchanges in accordance with best practices for systems engineering. This has resulted in the systems being vulnerable to exchanging incomplete or inaccurate data. Specifically, the PMO and FBI have designed the technical solutions for the NSI so that (1) users that submit ISE-SARs to Shared Spaces have the option to simultaneously submit them to eGuardian and (2) ISE-SARs that are submitted to eGuardian are automatically forwarded to the FBI's eGuardian Shared Spaces server, and are therefore available in both systems. In addition, all ISE-SARs submitted to eGuardian are automatically made available to the FBI's Guardian system and will be routed to a JTTF. To accomplish this, SARs are necessarily transferred between eGuardian and Shared Spaces, and between eGuardian and Guardian, as shown in figure 3.

When agencies electronically interconnect systems, if the interconnection is not properly designed and tested, it exposes the systems to technical risks that the data processed, stored, and transmitted may not be complete or accurate. In order to mitigate these risks, agencies should follow best practices when developing systems. NSI stakeholders have taken steps to facilitate the exchange of data among NSI systems, including the development of the ISE-SAR Information Exchange Package Document, which provides NSI participants with common definitions of terms used in an ISE-SAR. However, among other things, best practices also call for agencies to develop and implement testing criteria and plans based on technical requirements—considering the cost and complexity of testing the interconnection, and the criticality of doing so to the agencies' missions.[35] Such testing would help to identify any errors that may occur when transferring data over the interconnection and storing it in the receiving system, and would help ensure that information entered into Shared Spaces remains complete and accurate when it is transferred to and stored in eGuardian.[36]

See Appendix VI for additional information.

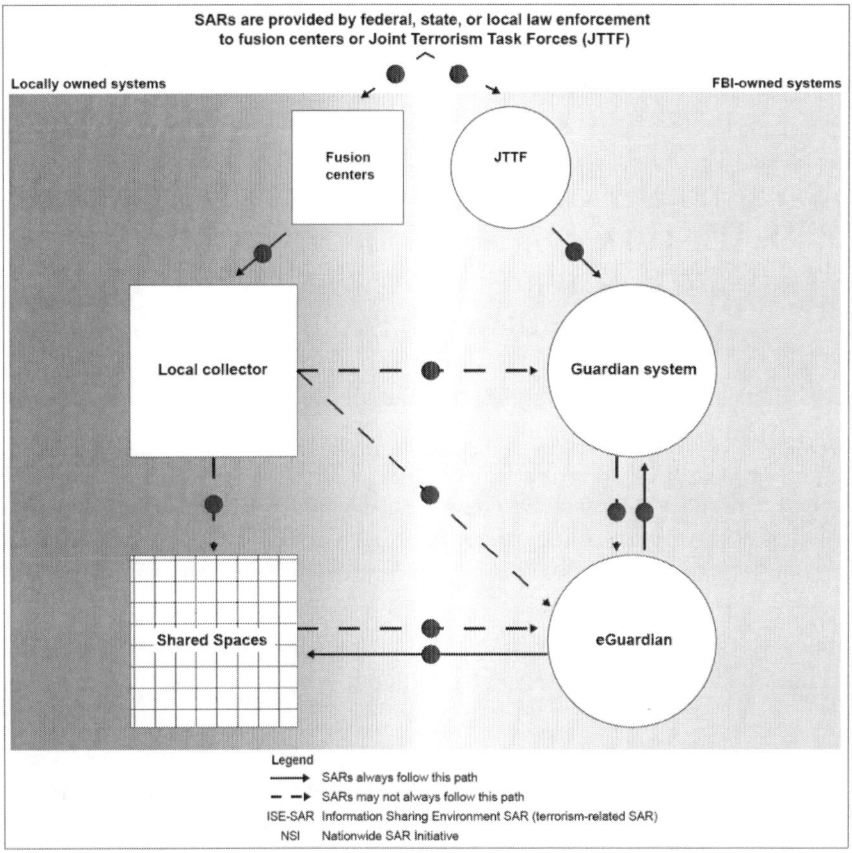

Source: GAO analysis of DOJ documents and interviews.

Figure 3. Suspicious Activity Report (SAR) Exchanges (Interoperability) among Shared Spaces, eGuardian, and Guardian.

PMO and FBI officials acknowledged that they did not take these steps, but rather they performed "ad hoc" testing after the systems were connected, correcting problems as they came up.[37] FBI officials said they did not fully follow best practices when establishing the interconnection between eGuardian and Shared Spaces because they wanted to rapidly establish this interconnection—and they would rather accept the risks associated with ad hoc testing than the risks associated with not receiving ISE-SARs that were entered into Shared Spaces. Although such a trade- off may have initially been necessary, without additional testing in accordance with best practices, the FBI cannot know what ISE-SAR information it is not receiving or be assured of the accuracy of the information that it does receive, which could affect its related threat assessments and investigations.

SELECTED STAKEHOLDERS REPORTED TRAINING TO DATE GENERALLY MET OBJECTIVES, BUT SOME TRAINING IS BEHIND SCHEDULE AND HAS NOT BEEN FULLY ASSESSED

NSI stakeholders we interviewed generally reported that training to date fully or partially met objectives. The PMO has established mechanisms to assess the fusion center analyst training to help ensure that all analysts are receiving the information they need to participate in the NSI. However, the PMO has not assessed its line officer training. The PMO has provided training to about 290,000 of the 800,000 line officers; 2,000 analytical personnel; and executives at 77 fusion centers.[38] The PMO is behind schedule in providing training to the line officers and is taking actions to provide training to those officers who have not yet received the training.

Stakeholders We Interviewed Generally Reported That Training Enhanced Their Ability to Contribute to the NSI

NSI stakeholders we interviewed about training—including senior officials at 7 fusion centers, line officers at 5 local police departments, and analysts at 7 fusion centers—generally reported that the training fully or partially met all of its objectives or effectively focused on its target areas.[39] For example, fusion center executives we interviewed generally reported that the executive training—an in-person briefing provided to fusion center executives before they agree to join the NSI—effectively focused on the role of the executive in leading implementation and steps for conducting community outreach. Line officers generally reported that the line officer training—a 15-minute video available on DVD or online— increased their awareness of the NSI and helped them to recognize incidents that could lead to a terrorist act. For instance, one local law enforcement officer said that a scene in the line officer training of a routine traffic stop that revealed a person with fireworks and pipes in the car demonstrated the importance of officers assessing the totality of information in a given situation to determine whether it should be documented as a terrorism-related ISE-SAR.

Also, the analysts we interviewed generally reported that the analyst training—an in-person 8-hour course—enhanced their ability to recognize terrorism-related SARs that they may not have identified as such prior to the training. Further, NSI stakeholders generally noted that the training enhanced their ability to avoid reporting SARs that are not terrorism- related. For example, an analyst from 1 fusion center said that the training helped clarify when an individual taking a picture or videotaping infrastructure is potentially terrorism-related and an ISE-SAR should be submitted versus a person taking pictures because the infrastructure is a tourist attraction. Finally, NSI stakeholders reported that the training enhanced analysts' or line officers' ability to protect privacy and civil liberties when vetting or documenting SARs.

PMO Assesses Analyst Training to Make Improvements but Does Not Assess Line Officer Training to Achieve Similar Benefits

The PMO has established mechanisms to obtain feedback on the training it provides to analysts at fusion centers and other agencies and uses this information to assess the training and make adjustments to improve it. Specifically, the PMO utilizes a survey to obtain written feedback on the training immediately following the training session, conducts assessments of participants' learning before and after the training, and obtains feedback on the training 90 days after it occurs. PMO survey results show that from January 2009 to July 2012, approximately 94 percent (1,273 of 1,342) of analysts rated the training as excellent or good and about 97 percent (1,279 of 1,316) reported that the training would help them apply the Functional Standard criteria to vet SARs.[40] The PMO also received input on how to further enhance the training, and incorporated suggestions. For instance, PMO officials reported that on the basis of this feedback, they adjusted the sequencing of the training segments and incorporated improved scenarios, using examples of actual ISE-SARs. This is consistent with factors we have previously reported that managers should consider when assessing agency training efforts.[41] One such factor is the collection of data corresponding to the established training objectives during the training's implementation, such as feedback on how well training programs are working and whether adjustments may be needed. Another factor is the use of appropriate analytical approaches to assess training, such as measures of training participants' reactions to, and satisfaction with, the training, or measures of changes in knowledge, skills, and abilities.

According to PMO officials, fusion center executives informally provide feedback both during the executive training and through interactions with PMO staff, which the officials said occurs frequently. They noted that the executive training is designed to provide an overview of the NSI and obtain the executive's agreement to participate in the initiative. Accordingly, PMO officials said that they assess the training based on whether the executives elect to participate in the NSI after receiving the training, and 74 of the 78 fusion centers are participating.

PMO officials said that they have not established a formal feedback mechanism for the line officer training, which could help ensure that the PMO's training provides the officers with sufficient information to enable them to identify and report terrorism-related suspicious activity that could help detect and prevent terrorist threats. This is because, according to PMO officials, the training is largely provided during routine agency roll call meetings in which many line officers view the training at one time, which makes it difficult for the PMO to ask the officers to complete a survey by hand or electronically. However, DHS has collected feedback through a one-page survey on some of its informational ISE-SAR materials that are meant to be distributed to law enforcement officers during roll call meetings.

According to PMO officials, line officers can also provide informal feedback on the training through the PMO's website. However, the line officer training does not include information that makes officers aware of this feedback option. Further, the website feedback mechanism does not include any specific questions about the training or how to improve it that would allow the PMO to assess or enhance it. Two of the online training providers have established their own feedback survey for line officers, and PMO officials said they review the survey responses. However, these surveys also do not ask specific questions related to the training objectives that would allow the PMO to determine how well the training is working or how to improve it. For example, the surveys only ask for a general rating of the content and do not ask questions that could help the PMO determine whether line officers have the information they need to perform their important role in identifying and reporting terrorism-related suspicious activity.

The officers from the five agencies we interviewed suggested that the training could provide information on current trends in terrorism, discuss the types of infrastructure and organizations that may be targeted by terrorists, specify what information should be included in an ISE-SAR, and include a quiz to test for understanding of the training materials, among other things. PMO officials said they planned to improve their efforts to review feedback on the line officer training, but they did not provide information on whether the PMO was going to solicit additional feedback or its approach for assessing the training. Taking additional steps to collect feedback from line officers could help the PMO improve its training to better help line officers fulfill their critical role in the NSI.

PMO Has Made Progress in Training Executives, Analysts, and Line Officers but Fell Short of Its Line Officer Goals; Stakeholders Are Taking Actions to Train More Officers

The PM-ISE has emphasized the importance of training executives, analysts, and line officers, and recommended that all agencies that participate in the NSI receive training. As of February 2013, the PMO had provided executive-level briefings to 77 of the 78 fusion centers and training to 2,000 analysts across the country. As most fusion centers are already participating in the NSI and have at least 1 analyst trained, PMO officials said that they are providing executive briefings and analyst trainings on an ongoing basis as needed to inform executives of NSI efforts and ensure that each fusion center continues to have at least 1 analyst trained.

As of February 2013, PMO data show that over 290,000 line officers had received training. However, this is about 64 percent short of the NSI's goal to train all line officers in the country (about 800,000) by the end of 2011. Officials from the PMO and organizations involved in developing the training—such as the International Association of Chiefs of Police— cited a number of challenges to providing this training. These include competing priorities of police departments, high turnover among line officers, difficulty reaching small and decentralized law enforcement entities, and the small number of PMO staff available to support training efforts. In addition, PMO officials explained that obtaining data on the number of line officers trained can be challenging, as they rely on police departments to report that number. The officials noted that the number reported is likely lower than the actual number of officers trained, although they acknowledged they have not reached all of the approximately 800,000 officers.

The PMO is taking actions to provide training to the remaining line officers. Specifically, PMO officials reported that they have been working with law enforcement entities to include the training as part of the entities' new officer training. PMO officials also said that they have worked with national law enforcement associations, such as the National Sheriffs' Association, to have the associations place a link to the line officer training on their websites. In addition, PMO officials reported that they have worked with the International Association of Chiefs of Police to reinvigorate the training efforts in five states, which, according to association officials, were chosen because of the relatively low percentage of officers that had completed the training, the presence of strong state police associations, and a large number of line officers. PMO officials said that they have seen an increase in the number of line officers trained in these states.

ISE-SARs Are Increasingly Being Used to Support Investigations and Analysis, but the PMO Is Not Measuring the Homeland Security Results Achieved

The PMO, FBI, and DHS have undertaken efforts to collect data on the number of ISE-SARs submitted, FBI investigations initiated based on ISE-SARs, and the potential usefulness of ISE-SARs in analyzing threat trends. These data show that NSI participants are increasingly using ISE- SARs, but do not track what difference the ISE-SARs have made, for example, in terms of their role in deterring terrorist activities or the number of arrests or convictions achieved. Such measures of results could provide decision makers with information on the program's impact on homeland security.

Available Data Show Stakeholders Have Increasingly Used the NSI to Investigate and Analyze ISE-SARs

Available data show that the number of ISE-SARs shared through the NSI and the number of FBI investigations based on ISE-SARs increased from fiscal years 2010 to 2012, and stakeholders have begun analyzing these ISE-SARs to identify patterns and trends posing security concerns. Specifically, according to PMO data, the number of ISE-SARs available to NSI participants in eGuardian and Shared Spaces has increased more than 750 percent from 3,256 in January 2010 to 27,855 in October 2012. According to PMO data, as of December 2012, the most frequent categories of suspicious activity reported were observation/surveillance; expressed or implied threat; sector-specific incident involving personnel, facilities, systems or functions; and theft/loss/diversion.[42] The number of terrorism investigations the FBI initiated based on these ISE-SARs also increased by about 75 percent from fiscal years 2010 to 2012. According to FBI data, there have been more than 1,200 investigations initiated as of September 2012 (see figure 4).[43]

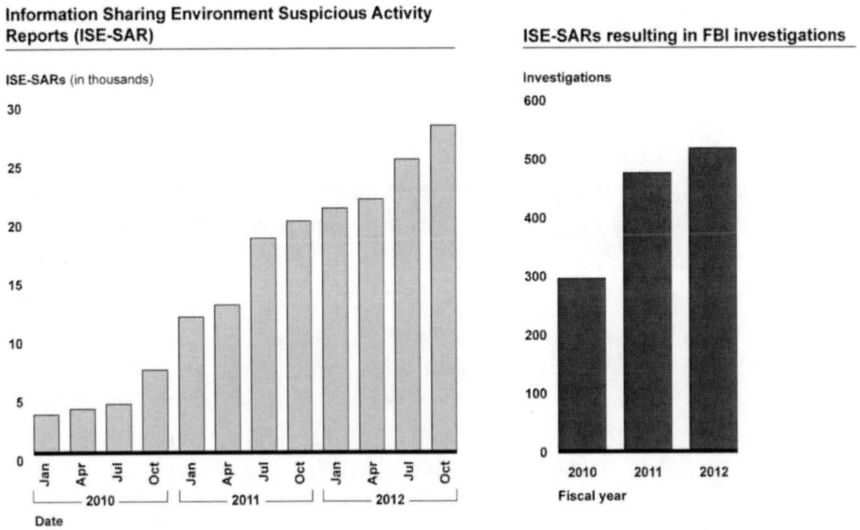

Source: GAO analysis of PMO and FBI data.

Note: Fiscal year 2012 investigations include data from October 1, 2011, through September 8, 2012.

Figure 4. Terrorism-Related Suspicious Activity Reports and Resulting FBI Investigations.

According to FBI officials, in general, the data reflect growth of the NSI and enhanced support from federal, state, and local partners in identifying potentially terrorism-related activity. The FBI does not systematically track the number of ISE-SARs that have helped inform actions to deter terrorist threats or led to arrests or convictions because investigations are tracked in a different system and are not specifically linked to ISE-SARs. However, the FBI and PMO are anecdotally aware of some ISE-SARs that have led to arrests or enhanced already existing FBI investigations. For example, the 2011 NSI annual report includes information on an incident in July 2011 where two U.S. Marines reported that while they were traveling in a government vehicle in Seattle, Washington, a male motorist appeared to look at their vehicle's government license plate, and then attempted to run them off the road. The Marines reported the incident to their commanding officer, and the information was ultimately forwarded to the Washington State Fusion Center and the Seattle Division JTTF. The FBI had a related, existing investigation that showed the motorist had recently been in contact with an individual who was charged in a foiled Seattle terrorism plot in June 2011 to attack a Seattle military facility. The motorist was arrested in September 2011 and charged with assaulting the Marines. DHS I&A has taken steps to determine the extent to which ISE-SARs could be or are used in analysis and found that most ISE-SARs reviewed contained information that could inform analysis and that NSI stakeholders are analyzing ISE-SARs to identify trends posing security concerns. For example, DHS I&A evaluated a sample of 3,044 ISE-SARs filed between January 2007 and December 2011 to determine the extent to which they were useful or had the potential for use in intelligence products, based on the ISE-SAR meeting the Functional Standard criteria, including information that would help identify a person or a location or address of the incident, or including a detailed description of the incident. I&A concluded that 69 percent of the ISE-SARs evaluated were useful or potentially useful, and found that the percentage of such ISE-SARs increased over time—from 66 percent in 2008 to 72 percent in 2011. PMO officials said that this analysis indicates that ISE-SARs shared through the NSI are of high quality and have analytic value.

DHS I&A also conducted a survey in April 2011 to determine the extent to which federal, state, local, tribal, and territorial agencies used ISE-SARs to develop analytical products. I&A found that in addition to the periodic products it develops, (1) the FBI, U.S. Coast Guard, Transportation Security Administration, and National Protection and Programs Directorate have developed ISE-SAR-based products, and (2) state, local, tribal, and territorial agencies have developed numerous products, the frequency and scope of which varied by region.[44] Such products included I&A's "Roll Call Releases," which use actual ISE-SARs to illustrate how agencies should apply the Functional Standard criteria, such as eliciting information on the purpose, operations, or security procedures of a facility that could be a potential target of a terrorist attack. Fusion centers have also developed products, such as the New Jersey Regional Operations Intelligence Center's quarterly reports, which identify trends in suspicious activity reporting in the state of New Jersey to help law enforcement focus resources on potential threats.

On the basis of the April 2011 survey results, I&A recommended that federal entities (1) provide additional support to fusion centers in regions with low analytical production and (2) increase the frequency of analytical products that focus on threats, such as threats to critical infrastructure, within specific geographic areas. In response, officials said I&A created the Field Analytic Support Taskforce in October 2012 to support state, local, and tribal intelligence requirements—including SARs—and facilitate regional collaboration among I&A analysts and federal interagency partners to identify, develop, and share intelligence products. PMO data show that ISE-SAR analysis may be increasing, as the number of Federated Search queries to review ISE-SAR data in Shared Spaces and eGuardian has increased from about 2,800 queries as of July 2010 to more than 71,000 queries as of February 2013.

PMO Has Not Established Plans or Time Frames for Implementing Measures That Assess the Homeland Security Benefits Derived from the NSI

The data above provide useful information on the outputs of the NSI, such as the number of ISE-SARs submitted and investigations initiated. However, they do not demonstrate results-oriented outcomes of ISE- SARs—such as the results of investigations or analysis, including arrests, convictions, or thwarted threats. Such information could help decision makers compare benefits achieved from investments in the NSI, and determine any needed changes to the process. In February 2010, the PM-ISE recommended that the PMO establish a performance measurement plan that includes a results-oriented approach and mature indicators that would provide information as to whether the ISE-SARs produced and shared under the program are meaningful and help achieve the objective of ensuring the "dots are connected" as well as optimize resources and promote accountability.[45] The PMO has not yet developed such a plan or related performance measures that would allow it to assess the results and homeland security benefits of the NSI. PMO officials said that they are working with subject matter experts to fulfill the PM-ISE's recommendation and that the experts were trying to develop metrics aimed at measuring terrorism prevention. However, PMO officials noted that defining such measures was difficult and did not demonstrate what progress had been made in developing such measures. Further, the officials could not provide a time frame for completing the performance measurement plan because they could not ensure the consistent involvement of one of the requisite experts.

We have recognized and reported that it is difficult to develop performance measures that show how certain information-sharing efforts have affected homeland security.[46] However, we have also reported that some agencies have made significant progress toward establishing such measures. For example, in October 2012, we reported that DHS's U.S. Customs and Border Protection had established performance measures to help it assess its approach for identifying maritime cargo shipments that may contain terrorist weapons or other contraband for further examination.[47] We recommended that the agency further strengthen its performance measures by establishing targets to regularly assess effectiveness and DHS concurred. Standard practices for program management call for specific desired outcomes or results to be conceptualized and defined in the planning process as part of a road map, along with milestones.[48] Developing ways to measure results beyond the number of investigations or agencies performing analysis would help the PMO determine the extent to which the NSI is achieving intended results and identify needed improvements. In the approximately 3 years since the PM-ISE recommended that the PMO establish a performance management plan that includes a results-oriented approach and related measures, the PMO has not been able to demonstrate progress toward this goal. Without establishing plans and time frames for implementing measures, the PMO and PM-ISE lack a means for establishing accountability for ensuring measures are implemented.

CONCLUSION

Analyzing and disseminating terrorism-related information in a timely manner is critical to the government's efforts to detect and prevent terrorist attacks. The NSI is a key program to address information-sharing challenges and was designed to establish a nationwide capability to collect and share terrorism-related ISE-SARs among federal, state, and local law enforcement.

Stakeholders generally reported that the NSI process is working well. However, formalizing mechanisms to provide stakeholders with feedback on the SARs they submit—which could include leveraging existing feedback mechanisms, such as those in eGuardian—and informing them of these mechanisms would be consistent with the PM-ISE recommendation and could help ensure that stakeholders receive the information they need to enforce SAR policies designed to protect privacy, maintain situational awareness, conduct accurate analyses, and motivate personnel to continue to report SARs.

Further, maintaining two systems to share ISE-SARs that provide duplicative services introduces risks identified by FBI officials that not all ISE-SAR information that should be shared is being shared or that the information that is shared remains complete and accurate when transferred between systems. The FBI and PMO have not identified the barriers that may prevent all ISE-SARs submitted to Shared Spaces from also being submitted to eGuardian or tested the interconnection between their respective systems to help ensure that the automatic exchange of ISE-SARs between the systems is complete and accurate. Without addressing these risks, the FBI cannot have reasonable assurance that it is receiving all ISE-SAR information that could help it investigate and prevent terrorist attacks. In addition, while the PMO assesses training for analysts and makes needed improvements based on assessment results, it has not developed or leveraged existing mechanisms to assess line officer training. Thus, the PMO lacks the ability to ensure that its training is effectively enabling line officers to perform their critical role in identifying and reporting on suspicious activities that may be related to terrorism. Finally, the PMO has taken steps to collect some data on the NSI. But until the PMO establishes a performance management plan that includes measures that assess what difference the ISE-SARs are making in terms of thwarting threats or resulting in arrests or convictions, for example, as well as plans and time frames for implementing the measures, the PMO and PM-ISE lack a means for establishing accountability for ensuring measures are implemented. Also, without such measures, decision makers cannot determine the extent to which the NSI is achieving intended homeland security results compared with investments made or identify and make needed improvements.

RECOMMENDATIONS FOR EXECUTIVE ACTION

To help ensure that the NSI is effectively implemented and that investments are achieving desired results, we recommend that the PMO, in consultation with the PM-ISE, FBI, fusion centers, and other relevant stakeholders take the following three actions:

- implement formalized mechanisms as part of the NSI to provide stakeholders feedback on the SARs they submit, consistent with the PM-ISE recommendation, and inform stakeholders of these mechanisms;
- develop or enhance existing mechanisms to assess the line officer training in order to ensure that it meets training objectives and identify and make improvements; and
- establish plans and time frames for developing and implementing a performance management plan, including measures that assess what difference ISE-SARs are making and the homeland security results achieved.

To mitigate risks associated with having two systems for collecting and sharing ISE-SARs, we recommend that the Attorney General task the PMO and FBI to take the following two actions:

- identify individual fusion centers' concerns that prevent them from always submitting ISE-SARs to eGuardian consistent with the Deputy Attorney General's December 2011 memorandum, and establish steps to address these concerns—as well as time frames for implementing the steps; and
- develop and implement testing criteria and plans based on technical requirements, consistent with best practices—considering the cost and complexity of the testing, and criticality of the interconnection to the agencies' missions—to help ensure that the automatic exchange of data between Shared Spaces and eGuardian is complete and accurate.

AGENCY COMMENTS AND OUR EVALUATION

We provided a draft of this report for review and comment to DOJ, DHS, and the PM-ISE. DOJ and DHS provided written comments. DOJ agreed with all five recommendations and identified actions taken or planned to implement them.

DOJ agreed with the first recommendation, that the PMO implement formalized mechanisms as part of the NSI to provide stakeholders feedback on the SARs they submit and inform stakeholders of these mechanisms. DOJ stated that the FBI currently provides feedback to SAR submitters through the eGuardian system and noted that the PMO is working with the FBI to make this feedback available in Shared Spaces. In addition, DOJ stated that the PMO will help fusion centers develop mechanisms to provide feedback to the reporting agency. If fully implemented, DOJ's planned efforts will address the intent of this recommendation.

DOJ agreed with the second recommendation, that the PMO develop or enhance existing mechanisms to assess the line officer training. DOJ stated that it is taking steps to solicit feedback through the online version of the line officer training and may take additional steps, if funding is available. If fully implemented, DOJ's planned efforts will address the intent of this recommendation.

DOJ agreed with the third recommendation, that the PMO establish plans and time frames for developing and implementing a performance management plan, including measures that assess what difference ISE- SARs are making and homeland security results achieved. DOJ stated that the PMO will work with the FBI, PM-ISE, and DHS to identify such metrics and will reinvigorate efforts to measure terrorism prevention. The extent to which DOJ's planned actions will fully address the intent of this recommendation will not be known until the agency completes its plans and establishes time frames for implementing them. We will continue to monitor the PMO's efforts.

DOJ agreed with the fourth recommendation, that the Attorney General task the PMO and FBI to identify individual fusion centers' concerns that prevent them from always submitting ISE-SARs to eGuaridan and establish steps to address these concerns and time frames for implementing the steps. DOJ stated that since January 2013, an additional 21 fusion centers had begun automatically sharing ISE-SARs with eGuardian. DOJ noted that of the remaining 7 fusion centers that were not automatically sharing ISE-SARs with eGuardian, 3 centers were submitting them electronically to eGuardian through other means,1 center had temporarily suspended automatic submissions until a technical issue was corrected on their local server, 1 center had recently agreed to implement automatic sharing and was in the process of doing so, and 2 centers had identified legal issues that prevented them from adopting the automatic sharing solution. DOJ stated that PMO and FBI officials were involved in ongoing discussions with the leadership of the 2 fusion centers that raised legal concerns to identify what steps could be taken to mitigate those concerns. We recognize the significant progress the PMO and FBI have made in addressing this recommendation and will continue to monitor their progress in working with the remaining fusion centers to identify and address concerns.

DOJ agreed with the fifth recommendation, that the Attorney General task the PMO and FBI to develop and implement testing criteria and plans, consistent with best practices, to help ensure that the automatic exchange of data between Shared Spaces and eGuardian is complete and accurate. DOJ stated that the PMO and FBI are currently working together to develop a common understanding of the requirements for a formal, repeatable testing protocol. In addition, DOJ stated that the FBI plans to implement a technical solution by April 2013 to automatically notify the PMO when SARs that are submitted to Shared Spaces are not received by the FBI through eGuardian. If fully implemented, DOJ's planned efforts will address the intent of this recommendation.

DOJ, DHS, and the PM-ISE also provided technical comments, which we incorporated in the report as appropriate.

Eileen R. Larence
Director
Homeland Security and Justice Issues

APPENDIX I. SCOPE AND METHODOLOGY

The objectives of this report were to evaluate (1) the progress federal agencies have made to implement the Nationwide Suspicious Activity Reporting Initiative (NSI), and what, challenges remain, if any; (2) the extent to which the technical means by which NSI stakeholders use to collect and share terrorism-related Suspicious Activity Reports (SAR) overlap or duplicate each other and introduce risks of these SARs not being shared; (3) the extent to which the NSI training has met its objectives, the NSI Program Management Office (PMO) is assessing the training, and the training has been completed; and (4) the extent to which the PMO has assessed how well the NSI is working and the homeland security results it has achieved.

To address these objectives, we reviewed NSI programmatic documents, such as the NSI concept of operations and annual reports, and obtained and analyzed Department of Justice (DOJ) data, including data regarding NSI implementation, training, costs, and results—from the inception of the PMO in fiscal years 2010 through 2012. We also interviewed officials from the Program Manager for the Information Sharing Environment (PM-ISE), DOJ, and the Department of Homeland Security (DHS) who are responsible for overseeing NSI efforts.[49] We obtained information from DOJ officials who manage the data about the steps taken to ensure their accuracy, and found the data to be sufficiently reliable for the purposes of this report.

In addition, to address the first three objectives, we interviewed nonprobability samples of officials from entities participating in the NSI, including officials from seven fusion centers—state- or locally- operated entities that serve as the focal point within a state or major urban area for sharing and analyzing threat information.[50] The seven fusion centers were the Boston Regional Intelligence Center, the Chicago Crime Prevention and Information Center, the Colorado Information Analysis Center, the Minnesota Joint Analysis Center, the New York State Intelligence Center, the Nevada Threat Analysis Center, and the Virginia Fusion Center.

These fusion centers were selected based upon criteria designed to get a range of perspectives and experiences, which included geographic location, whether the center served an urban area, when the center received training, and level of participation in the NSI. To better understand concerns regarding the potential impact of the NSI on privacy, we selected four fusion centers that the PMO indicated had expressed some concerns with using eGuardian as a primary means of sharing SARs through the NSI. At each of the seven fusion centers, we interviewed executives—six of whom had received NSI training designed for executives—analysts who had received NSI analytical training, and officials who were familiar with their entities' systems for documenting and sharing SARs.

To address the first three objectives, we also interviewed a nonprobability sample of Federal Bureau of Investigation (FBI) officials who are responsible for investigating and analyzing terrorism-related SARs from seven field offices in the following locations that were proximal to the fusion centers we reviewed: Albany, New York; Boston, Massachusetts; Chicago, Illinois; Denver, Colorado; Minneapolis, Minnesota; Reno, Nevada; and Richmond, Virginia. When possible, we interviewed officials from local law enforcement agencies in proximity to the fusion centers we reviewed that had taken the line officer training. We met with officials from five local law enforcement agencies, including the Andover, Massachusetts, Police Department; Carson City, Nevada, Sheriff's Department; Highland Park, Illinois, Police Department; Minneapolis, Minnesota, Police Department; and the Norfolk, Virginia, Police Department. At all five law enforcement agencies, we met with officials who had taken the NSI training designed for line officers and who were responsible for reviewing SARs. To obtain perspectives from participating federal agencies, we met with officials from the Federal Protective Service and the Bureau of Alcohol, Tobacco, Firearms and Explosives, which were selected based upon having a relatively high number of officers who had received NSI training. Although the views of the individuals in our samples provide valuable insight into the implementation of the NSI, they are not generalizable to all federal, state, and local entities participating in the NSI. Other homeland security partners—such as critical infrastructure owners and operators, firefighters, and private security professionals—have begun to participate in the NSI. We did not include these entities in our work because their training just began in April 2012.

We took additional steps to address the second, third, and fourth objectives regarding NSI technology, training, and results, respectively.

To address the second question, we reviewed DOJ documentation regarding the two systems for collecting, sharing, and analyzing SARs, such as user manuals, implementation guides, and privacy impact assessments.[51] We compared the services of each system to determine the extent to which they overlap or duplicate and assessed the extent to which DOJ followed best practices for ensuring the systems effectively exchange information.[52] To address the third question, we reviewed and assessed PMO documentation regarding training objectives, targets, and recipient feedback mechanisms using leading practices for training programs.[53] To address the fourth question, we assessed the PMO's plans for measuring the results the NSI has achieved using best practices for program management.[54]

We conducted this performance audit from February 2012 to March 2013 in accordance with generally accepted government auditing standards. Those standards require that we plan and perform the audit to obtain sufficient, appropriate evidence to provide a reasonable basis for our findings and conclusions based on our audit objectives. We believe that the evidence we obtained provides a reasonable basis for our findings and conclusions based on our audit objectives.

Appendix II. Functional Standard Terrorism-Related SAR Criteria Guidance

The ISE-SAR Functional Standard was first issued by the Program Manager for the Information Sharing Environment in January 2008 and updated in May 2009, and defines common processes for collecting and sharing suspicious activity reports with a potential nexus to terrorism. Pursuant to a two-part process outlined in the Functional Standard, SARs that are determined to have a potential nexus to terrorism are known as ISE-SARs. The Functional Standard includes business rules and formats for exchanging ISE-SARs that were agreed to by both operating organizations (frontline law enforcement) and privacy and civil liberties advocacy groups. The Functional Standard has been designed to incorporate key elements that describe potential criminal activity associated with terrorism, as shown in table 3 below.

Table 3. Functional Standard ISE-SAR Criteria Guidance

Defined criminal activity and potential terrorism nexus activity	
Breach/attempted intrusion	Unauthorized personnel attempting to or actually entering a restricted area or protected site. Impersonation of authorized personnel (e.g., police/security, janitor).
Misrepresentation	Presenting false or misusing insignia, documents, or identification to misrepresent one's affiliation to cover possible illicit activity.
Theft/loss/diversion	Stealing or diverting something associated with a facility/infrastructure (e.g., badges, uniforms, identification, emergency vehicles, technology, or documents [classified or unclassified], which are proprietary to the facility).
Sabotage/tampering/ vandalism	Damaging, manipulating, or defacing part of a facility/infrastructure or protected site.
Cyber attack	Compromising, or attempting to compromise or disrupt an organization's information technology infrastructure.
Expressed or implied threat	Communicating a spoken or written threat to damage or compromise a facility/infrastructure.
Aviation activity	Operation of an aircraft in a manner that reasonably may be interpreted as suspicious, or posing a threat to people or property. Such operation may or may not be a violation of Federal Aviation Regulations.
Potential criminal or noncriminal activity requiring additional fact information during investigation[a]	
Eliciting information	Questioning individuals acting at a level beyond mere curiosity about particular facets of a facility's or building's purpose, operations, security procedures, and so forth that would arouse suspicion in a reasonable person.
Testing or probing of security	Deliberate interactions with, or challenges to, installations, personnel, or systems that reveal physical, personnel, or cyber security capabilities.
Recruiting	Building of operations teams and contacts, personnel data, banking data, or travel data.

Table 3. (Continued)

Potential criminal or noncriminal activity requiring additional fact information during investigation[a]	
Photography	Taking pictures or video of facilities, buildings, or infrastructure in a manner that would arouse suspicion in a reasonable person. Examples include taking pictures or video of infrequently used access points, personnel performing security functions (patrols, badge/vehicle checking), security- related equipment (perimeter fencing, security cameras), and so forth.
Observation/ surveillance	Demonstrating unusual interest in facilities, buildings, or infrastructure beyond mere casual or professional (e.g., engineers') interest such that a reasonable person would consider the activity suspicious. Examples include observation through binoculars, taking notes, attempting to measure distances, and so forth.
Materials acquisition/storage	Acquisition or storage of unusual quantities of materials such as cell phones, pagers, fuel, chemicals, toxic materials, and timers, such that a reasonable person would suspect possible criminal activity.
Acquisition of expertise	Attempts to obtain or conduct training in security concepts, military weapons or tactics, or other unusual capabilities that would arouse suspicion in a reasonable person.
Weapons discovery	Discovery of unusual amounts of weapons or explosives that would arouse suspicion in a reasonable person.
Sector-specific incident	Actions associated with a characteristic of unique concern to specific sectors (such as the public health sector) with regard to their personnel, facilities, systems, or functions.

Source: Program Manager for the Information Sharing Environment, Functional Standard v. 1.5, Part B.

[a] These activities are generally First Amendment-protected activities and should not be reported in a SAR or ISE (terrorism)-SAR absent articulable facts and circumstances that support the source agency's suspicion that the behavior observed is not innocent, but rather reasonably indicative of criminal activity associated with terrorism, including evidence of pre-operational planning related to terrorism.

Race, ethnicity, national origin, or religious affiliation should not be considered as factors that create suspicion (although these factors may be used as specific suspect descriptions).

APPENDIX III. FEDERAL AGENCIES PARTICIPATING IN THE NSI

As of November 2012, 53 federal agencies and over 300 Department of Defense (DOD) entities were participating in the NSI, according to the FBI.[55] Twenty-seven of these agencies are considered "NSI compliant" because they have met all NSI participation criteria, including receiving an executive-level briefing, entering into an agreement to participate in the NSI, establishing a SAR protocol, completing the frontline officer training and SAR analytic training, establishing a privacy policy, and obtaining an eGuardian account. The other 26 agencies are "NSI operational" and have met all of the above requirements, with the exception of completing the SAR analytical training. The compliant and operational agencies are listed below, along with their parent organizations, as applicable.

NSI Compliant:

Federal Bureau of Investigation (DOJ)
Bureau of Alcohol, Tobacco, Firearms and Explosives (DOJ)
U.S. Marshals Service (DOJ)
Drug Enforcement Agency (DOJ)
Bureau of Prisons (DOJ)
Office of Security Services (Department of Commerce)
National Park Service (Department of the Interior)
U.S. Park Police (Department of the Interior)
Treasury Inspector General for Tax Administration (Department of the Treasury)
Environmental Protection Agency
National Institutes of Health (Department of Health and Human Services)
Food and Drug Administration (Department of Health and Human Services)
National Aeronautics and Space Administration
Diplomatic Security Service (Department of State)
U.S. Agency for International Development
Federal Communications Commission
Government Printing Office
Office of Intelligence (Department of Energy)

Federal Air Marshal Service (DHS)
National Infrastructure Coordinating Center (DHS)
Federal Protective Service (DHS)
National Operations Center (DHS)
Federal Emergency Management Agency (DHS)
U.S. Customs and Border Protections (DHS)
U.S. Secret Service (DHS)
U.S. Immigration and Customs Enforcement (DHS)
U.S. Coast Guard (DHS)

Operational:

Nuclear Regulatory Commission (Department of Energy)
National Nuclear Security Administration (Department of Energy)
Office of Health Safety and Security (Department of Energy)
Bureau of Indian Affairs (Department of the Interior)
Bureau of Land Management (Department of the Interior)
Law Enforcement and Security Headquarters (Department of the Interior)
Bureau of Reclamation (Department of the Interior)
U.S. Fish and Wildlife Service (Department of the Interior)
U.S. Forest Service (Department of Agriculture)
National Zoological Park Police
Internal Revenue Service (Department of the Treasury)
U.S. Mint (Department of the Treasury)
U.S. Capitol Police
Office of Security Services (Department of Education)
Federal Investigative Services (Office of Personnel Management)
Federal Reserve Board
Office of Security and Emergency Management (Department of Labor)
U.S. Supreme Court
Inspector General (GAO)
Department of Veterans Affairs
Office of Security and Emergency Planning (Department of Housing and Urban Development)
U.S. Postal Inspector Service
Federal Aviation Administration (Department of Transportation)
Special Services Police (Central Intelligence Agency)
Tennessee Valley Authority
Amtrak

Appendix IV. Similar and Unique Services Provided by Shared Spaces and eGuardian

This appendix corresponds with figure 2 in the report.

Table 4. Similar Services Provided by Shared Spaces and eGuardian

Service provided by both	Shared Spaces implementation	eGuardian implementation
Access to submit ISE-SARs into nationwide network	Fusion centers and other entities with Shared Spaces servers have the ability to submit ISE- SARs into Shared Spaces.	The FBI allows all law enforcement entities across the country to create eGuardian accounts and submit ISE-SARs into eGuardian.
Access to review and analyze ISE- SARs others have submitted	Fusion centers and other entities with Shared Spaces servers have access to the Federated Search tool, which enables them to review and analyze ISE-SARs in Shared Spaces. Fusion center directors can allow local law enforcement entities to have access to the Federated Search also.	The FBI allows all law enforcement entities across the country to create eGuardian accounts and review and analyze ISE-SARs in eGuardian
Ability to share ISE-SAR information with the other system	Many ISE-SARs that are submitted to Shared Spaces are simultaneously submitted to eGuardian.	All ISE-SARs that are submitted to eGuardian are forwarded by the FBI to its Shared Spaces server, which is accessible to users of the Shared Spaces' Federated Search tool.
Search and analysis tools	Shared Spaces has several search and analysis features similar to those of eGuardian, and also has enhanced analytic capabilities, such as the ability to drill down and link common ISE-SAR elements.	eGuardian has several search and analysis features similar to those of Shared Spaces, and also allows users to generate exportable reports on a variety of ISE-SAR-related information.
Ability to submit ISE-SARs to FBI JTTFs and to Guardian (the FBI's classified counterterrorism incident management system)	When submitting ISE-SARs to Shared Spaces, users may also simultaneously send them to eGuardian, which then forwards the ISE-SARs to the appropriate JTTF and to Guardian.	All ISE-SARs submitted into eGuardian are automatically forwarded to the appropriate JTTF and to Guardian.

Table 4. (Continued)

Service provided by both	Shared Spaces implementation	eGuardian implementation
Ability to remove ISE-SARs from the NSI on demand	Shared Spaces enables ISE-SAR submitters to remove ISE-SARs at their discretion.	The FBI currently requires that ISE-SAR submitters contact the eGuardian help desk and request their ISE-SAR be removed; upon obtaining a reason for removal, the FBI will remove the ISE-SAR. The FBI is working on a feature that will make this process electronic.[a]

Source: GAO analysis of DOJ documents and interviews.

[a] In commenting on a draft of this report, FBI officials noted that in February 2013, the FBI implemented a new feature in eGuardian that allows fusion centers to directly and electronically remove their ISE-SARs.

Table 5. Unique Services Provided by Shared Spaces and eGuardian

Service provided by Shared Spaces	Service provided by eGuardian
Control over who can add information to ISE-SARs Only original ISE-SAR submitters can add information to ISE-SARs.	Ability for users other than the original ISE-SAR submitter to supplement ISE-SAR information. eGuardian allows users other than the original ISE-SAR submitter to "add notes" to ISE-SARs.
Control over who can download ISE-SARs For privacy reasons, Shared Spaces does not allow users to download ISE-SARs, but the NSI PMO is working on a "virtual download" feature that will enable users to temporarily download ISE-SARs into a controlled space for purposes of analysis.	Ability to access FBI feedback on ISE-SARs. eGuardian users are able to view the outcome of the FBI's threat assessment of the ISE-SAR, as well as access contact information for FBI personnel with knowledge of the ISE-SAR.

Service provided by Shared Spaces	Service provided by eGuardian
Greater control of the retention periods of ISE-SARs Fusion centers cannot retain ISE-SARs beyond 5 years unless the information is revalidated. However, many fusion centers have established shorter retention periods.	Ability to download ISE-SARs The FBI allows users to download ISE-SARs.
Ability to restrict certain data elements from broader view Fusion centers and other entities with Shared Spaces servers can select which data elements they want to be accessible to other users.	Fixed retention schedules for ISE-SARs in eGuardian and Guardian All ISE-SARs in eGuardian are retained for up to 5 years, unless the user removes the ISE-SAR. All ISE-SARs in eGuardian are also shared with Guardian, which has different retention policies. See appendix V for eGuardian and Guardian retention policies.
Ability to perform a Federated Search over all ISE-SARs in the NSI Users of Shared Spaces have access to the Federated Search tool, which enables them to search among ISE-SARs located on all Shared Spaces servers across the country, including the FBI's Shared Spaces server.	Ability to share information with the FBI but not with other users of eGuardian or Shared Spaces. eGuardian users have the ability to submit SARs or ISE-SARs directly to JTTFs and Guardian without sharing them more broadly with users of eGuardian or Shared Spaces
	Ability to request coordination with the FBI eGuardian users may check a box indicating they would like the FBI to contact them before the FBI does any investigative work related to their submission.

Source: GAO analysis of DOJ documents and interviews.

APPENDIX V. SAR RETENTION POLICIES IN THE FBI'S eGUARDIAN AND GUARDIAN SYSTEMS

SAR retention schedules are based on the outcome of the FBI's threat assessments for each SAR. Some SARs do not receive threat assessments as they are for information only, and their retention schedule is 5 years in eGuardian. The following table shows the retention schedules of SARs based on the outcome of their threat assessments.

Table 6. Retention Schedules for SARs in the FBI's eGuardian and Guardian Systems

FBI system	Outcome of FBI threat assessment		
	No nexus to terrorism	Inconclusive nexus to terrorism	Nexus to terrorism
eGuardian	Deleted after 180 days	Deleted after 5 years	Deleted after 5 years
	After deleted, retained in or by Guardian (see below) ACS/Sentinel (30 years) NARA	After deleted, retained in or by Guardian (see below) ACS/Sentinel (30 years) NARA	After deleted, retained in or by Guardian (see below) ACS/Sentinel (30 years) NARA
Guardian	Deleted after 5 Years	Deleted after 5 Years	Deleted after 5 Years
	If queried prior to deletion, then No change	If queried prior to deletion, then After 5 years, supervisor can view until 10 years, then deleted completely	If queried prior to deletion, then After 5 years, supervisor can view until 10 years, then deleted completely
	After deleted, retained in or by ACS/Sentinel (30 years) NARA	After deleted, retained in or by ACS/Sentinel (30 years) NARA	After deleted, retained in or by ACS/Sentinel (30 years) NARA

ACS: Automated Case Support system (the FBI's former cases management system)

Sentinel: The FBI's case support system they are transitioning to (FBI's current case management system)

NARA: National Archives Records Administration

Source: FBI.

APPENDIX VI. SAR EXCHANGES (INTEROPERABILITY) AMONG SHARED SPACES, EGUARDIAN, AND GUARDIAN

This appendix corresponds with figure 3 in the report.

Table 7. SAR Exchanges (Interoperability) among Shared Spaces, eGuardian, and Guardian

Element of figure	Associated text
SARs are provided by federal, state, or local law enforcement to fusion centers or JTTFs	
Dotted line going from statement above to fusion centers	Law enforcement agencies may provide SARs to fusion centers by a variety of means, such as telephone or e-mail, or by using eGuardian (SARs submitted using eGuardian remain in "draft" status and are not yet submitted as ISE-SARs to the broader eGuardian user base).
Dotted line going from statement above to JTTFs	Law enforcement agencies may provide SARs to JTTFs by a variety of means, such as telephone or e-mail, or by using the "eGuardian Express" feature within eGuardian (this feature enables them to submit SARs directly to the FBI that are not viewable to other eGuardian users).
Fusion centers	Fusion centers serve as focal points within the state and local environment for the receipt, analysis, gathering, and sharing of threat-related information among the federal government and state, local, tribal, territorial, and private sector partners.
FBI JTTFs	The FBI has established JTTFs to investigate terrorism-related activity.
Solid line going from fusion centers to local collector	Upon receiving SARs from law enforcement, fusion center personnel enter them into their local collector.
Solid line going from FBI JTTF to Guardian system	Upon receiving SARs from law enforcement, JTTF personnel enter them into Guardian.
Local collector	Each fusion center has a local collector where it stores SARs. These collectors may include commercial products, legacy systems, the SAR Vetting Tool (a software application developed by the NSI), or eGuardian (agencies may use eGuardian to store their SARs without disseminating them more broadly).

Table 7. (Continued)

Element of figure	Associated text
Guardian system	Guardian is the FBI's classified counterterrorism incident management system.
Shared Spaces	Shared Spaces is a collection of similarly configured servers that are owned and located locally, across the country, and searchable through a common portal called the Federated Search.
eGuardian	eGuardian is the FBI's unclassified system for sharing ISE-SARs.
Dotted line going from local collector to Guardian system	Fusion Centers can use eGuardian "web services" to electronically forward ISE-SARs from their local collectors to eGuardian. If doing so is desired, users may choose the "eGuardian Express" feature, which will ensure ISE-SARs are provided to Guardian and the appropriate JTTF, but are not viewable in eGuardian.
Dotted line going from local collector to eGuardian and solid line going from eGuardian to Shared Spaces	Fusion centers can use eGuardian "web services" to electronically forward ISE-SARs from their local collectors to eGuardian. They can also submit ISE-SARs directly to eGuardian using eGuardian's web interface. All ISE-SARs submitted to eGuardian are forwarded to the FBI's Shared Spaces server, which is accessible to users of Shared Spaces.
Dotted line going from local collector to Shared Spaces and from Shared Spaces to eGuardian	From their local collectors, fusion centers can electronically submit ISE-SARs to Shared Spaces only, or, using the SAR Vetting Tool developed by the NSI, they can submit their ISE-SARs to both Shared Spaces and eGuardian. If they choose to submit them to both systems, the ISE- SARs go first to Shared Spaces and are then forwarded to eGuardian.
Dotted line going from Guardian system to eGuardian	After SARs have been entered into Guardian by FBI personnel, unclassified information is generally shared with eGuardian.
Solid line going from eGuardian to Guardian system	All ISE-SARs submitted to eGuardian are shared with Guardian and the appropriate FBI JTTF.
Solid line going from eGuardian to Shared Spaces	All ISE-SARs in eGuardian are forwarded to the FBI's Shared Spaces server, and are accessible to users of Shared Spaces.

Source: GAO analysis of DOJ documents and interviews.

APPENDIX VII. COMMENTS FROM THE DEPARTMENT OF JUSTICE

U.S. Department of Justice

Washington, D.C. 20530

MAR - 1 2013

Ms. Eileen Larence
Director
Homeland Security and Justice Issues
Government Accountability Office
441 G Street, NW
Washington, DC 20548

Dear Ms. Larence:

Thank you for the opportunity to review and comment on the draft Government Accountability Office (GAO) report entitled, "*Information Sharing: Additional Actions Could Help Ensure That Efforts to Share Terrorism-Related Suspicious Activity Reports Are Effective*" (GAO-13-233). The Department of Justice (Department, DOJ) appreciates the work of the GAO and has carefully considered the findings and recommendations presented in GAO's draft report.

The Department established the Nationwide Suspicious Activity Reporting (SAR) Initiative (NSI) Program Management Office (NSI-PMO), within the Office of Justice Programs' Bureau of Justice Assistance (BJA) in March 2010. Since its establishment, the NSI-PMO has been working in partnership with the Federal Bureau of Investigation (FBI), the Program Manager for the Information Sharing Environment (PM-ISE), the Department of Homeland Security (DHS), and state, local, tribal, and territorial government partners to implement the standards, policies, processes, and technology necessary for law enforcement agencies to share suspicious activity reports that are potentially indicative of terrorism while ensuring the protection of privacy, civil rights, and civil liberties of all Americans. To date, implementation efforts have far outpaced original timelines of four to five years, with 74 fusion centers currently participating in the NSI, as of February 2013. The majority of these centers are able to immediately and seamlessly share SARs to both the NSI Federated Search (Shared Spaces), as well as with the FBI via the eGuardian system, ensuring that the FBI receives all SAR-related information for possible investigation.

Based on their findings, the draft GAO report contains five Recommendations for Executive Action to the DOJ, which are restated in bold text below and are followed by our response.

Ms. Eileen Larence 2

To help ensure that the NSI is effectively implemented and that investments are achieving desired results, we recommend that the PMO, in consultation with the PM-ISE, FBI, fusion centers, and other relevant stakeholders take the following three actions:

1. **Implement formalized mechanisms as part of the NSI to provide stakeholders feedback on the SARs they submit, consistent with the PM-ISE recommendation, and inform stakeholders of these mechanisms.**

   The Department agrees with this Recommendation. The FBI currently provides feedback through the eGuardian system to inform a SAR provider when information submitted in a SAR is used to open an FBI investigation or assist in enhancing an existing FBI investigation. The NSI PMO is working with the FBI to develop a technical solution to expand this capability to port this feedback into the Shared Space. In addition, the NSI PMO will provide support to fusion centers to help them develop a feedback mechanism from the fusion center to the reporting agency / officer.

2. **Develop or enhance existing mechanisms to assess the line officer training in order to ensure that it meets training objectives and identify and make improvements.**

   The Department agrees with this Recommendation. The NSI PMO has already taken steps to assess the line officer training, to include comprehension questions and information for feedback on the online version of the line officer training. In addition, if funding is available, the NSI PMO will explore the development of a standardized Peace Officer Standards and Training (POST) certified training, which would include the NSI line officer training. Because of the standards involved with obtaining POST training certification, this training would include comprehension questions and also provide a mechanism for officers to provide feedback.

3. **Establish plans and time frames for developing and implementing a performance management plan, including measures that assess what difference ISE-SARs are making and the homeland security results achieved.**

   The Department agrees with this Recommendation. The NSI PMO will work with the FBI, PM-ISE, and DHS to identify metrics that can illustrate the impact of NSI on homeland security to supplement reporting of the number of investigations opened or enhanced. While the Department is in the early stages of exploring these possibilities, such metrics could possibly include items such as the type of cases opened and the longer-term disposition of cases. In addition, NSI PMO will explore distilling existing metrics to the SAR provider level to display a more granular breakdown of the currently compiled number of investigations opened or enhanced. Finally, the NSI PMO will also reinvigorate their previous efforts to measure prevention, which were put on hold due to limited funding.

Ms. Eileen Larence 3

To mitigate risks associated with having two systems for collecting and sharing ISE-SARs, we recommend that the Attorney General task the PMO and FBI to take the following two actions:

4. Identify individual fusion centers' concerns that prevent them from always submitting ISE-SARs to eGuardian consistent with the Deputy Attorney General's December 2011 memorandum, and establish steps to address these concerns—as well as time frames for implementing the steps.

The Department agrees with this Recommendation. Since January 1, 2013, the auto-push function has been installed in 21 additional fusion centers. There are now only seven fusion centers that are not automatically pushing SARs to eGuardian. Of those seven, three are submitting the SARs electronically to eGuardian by alternate means; one center has temporarily suspended the automatic push until a technical issue is corrected on their local server; another center recently agreed to implement the automatic push and is in the process of doing so; and two centers have identified legal issues that prevent them from adopting the automatic push solution. OJP and FBI are involved in ongoing discussions with the leadership of the remaining two fusion centers that have raised legal concerns regarding sharing ISE-SAR information with the FBI electronically via eGuardian to determine what steps, if any, could be taken to mitigate those concerns.

5. Develop and implement testing criteria and plans based on technical requirements, consistent with best practices—considering the cost and complexity of the testing, and criticality of the interconnection to the agencies' missions—to help ensure that the automatic exchange of data between Shared Spaces and eGuardian is complete and accurate.

The Department agrees with this Recommendation. The NSI PMO and the FBI Guardian Management Unit are currently working to develop a common understanding of what is needed to establish a formal process based on the Department's Software Development Life Cycle standards and a repeatable testing protocol. In addition, technical staff, responsible for the Shared Spaces and eGuardian systems, have recognized the need for a common dedicated hardware and software environment to improve joint interoperability testing, as well as diagnostic support and issue resolution to ensure that overall system availability is maintained at a high level.

Further, the FBI has developed a web-based technical solution to notify the NSI PMO when SAR are pushed by fusion centers via the Shared Space are not received by the FBI, which triggers an immediate inquiry by the NSI PMO to troubleshoot the problem. This web-based solution is anticipated to be fully implemented by April 1, 2013. Currently this process is being tracked manually and the NSI-PMO generates a weekly dashboard which has identified only a few instances in which SAR were not received by the FBI. Once implemented, the web-based solution should prevent transmission failures of SAR from the Shared Spaces to eGuardian. However, with the complexity of the technology and the differences in the Shared Spaces and eGuardian systems, coordinated

Ms. Eileen Larence 4

efforts between the NSI PMO and the FBI are ongoing to ensure that all SAR reported by NSI participants are forwarded to eGuardian accurately and expeditiously in the future.

If I may be of further assistance to you, please do not hesitate to contact me. Your staff may also contact Richard Theis, Assistant Director, Audit Liaison Group on 202-307-0116.

Sincerely,

Lee J. Lofthus
Assistant Attorney General
for Administration

cc: Tony West
Acting Associate Attorney General
Office of the Associate Attorney General

Trisha Anderson
Senior Counsel to the Deputy Attorney General
Office of the Deputy Attorney General

Andrew G. McCabe
Assistant Director
Counterterrorism Division
Federal Bureau of Investigation

Laura R. Ingber
Section Chief, External Audit and Compliance Section
Inspection Division
Federal Bureau of Investigation

Mary Lou Leary
Acting Assistant Attorney General
Office of Justice Programs

James H. Burch, II
Deputy Assistant Attorney General
for Operations and Management
Office of Justice Programs

Denise O'Donnell
Director
Bureau of Justice Assistance
Office of Justice Programs

End Notes

[1] See, e.g., 6 U.S.C. § 485 (directing the President to create an information-sharing environment that, among other things, provides or supports a decentralized, distributed, and coordinated environment for sharing terrorism-related information), and Executive Office of the President, *National Strategy for Information Sharing: Successes and Challenges in Improving Terrorism-Related Information Sharing* (Washington D.C.: October 2007).

[2] In general, a SAR is official documentation of observed behavior reasonably indicative of preoperational planning related to terrorism or other criminal activity. The NSI facilitates the sharing of terrorism-related SARs.

[3] Terrorism-related information sharing remained a high-risk area for our February 2013 update. See GAO, *High-Risk Series: An Update*, GAO-13-283 (Washington, D.C.: Feb. 14, 2013) for the most recent update.

[4] The PM-ISE plans for, oversees implementation of, and manages the government-wide Information Sharing Environment (ISE)—an approach for sharing terrorism-related information that may include any method deemed necessary and appropriate. See 6 U.S.C. § 485(a)(3), (f).

[5] Unlike a random sample, a nonprobability sample is more deliberatively chosen, meaning that some elements of the population being studied have either no chance or an unknown chance of being selected as part of the sample. Appendix I contains more information on the rationales we used to choose our samples.

[6] Best practices are included in DOJ, *The Department of Justice Systems Development Life Cycle Guidance Document* (Washington D.C.: January 2003).

[7] See, for example, GAO, *Human Capital: A Guide for Assessing Strategic Training and Development Efforts in the Federal Government*, GAO-04-546G (Washington D.C.: March 2004).

[8] The Project Management Institute, *The Standard for Program Management* © (Newton Square, PA: 2006).

[9] PM-ISE, *ISE Functional Standard: Suspicious Activity Reporting, Version 1.5*, ISE-FS-200 (Washington D.C.: May 21, 2009). Appendix II contains additional information on the Functional Standard.

[10] According to FBI officials, the FBI uses the criteria in the eGuardian Privacy Impact Assessment (dated November 25, 2008) and the FBI's Domestic Investigations and Operations Guide to determine if SARs have a potential nexus to terrorism. The officials said that these criteria are generally consistent with the Functional Standard and the FBI and PMO are taking steps to further harmonize the criteria.

[11] PMO officials noted that Shared Spaces could also be used to share other types of criminal information, such as gang-related data. The PM-ISE has recommended that DOJ examine the potential for using Shared Spaces to share critical information on other priority threats and crimes. The PM-ISE noted that, as of December 2012, DOJ had not yet submitted an implementation plan for such an approach.

[12] When law enforcement agencies submit SARs through eGuardian, personnel at the area fusion center or the FBI's "eFusion center" vet the SAR against the Functional Standard or an equivalent standard before the SAR is disseminated within eGuardian for broader viewing.

[13] Additional information on which entities use Shared Spaces servers and which use eGuardian is discussed later in this report.

[14] The federal agencies participating in the NSI include independent federal agencies and government corporations.

[15] Officials from the remaining fusion center said they did not know if the process was working well. An official from the remaining local agency said that the process was not working well and that the agency needed additional information to ensure that all officers know to whom to provide SAR information.

[16] Analysts from the remaining fusion center said that feedback was not that important because their job is just to make sure that the FBI receives the information.

[17] PM-ISE, *Nationwide Suspicious Activity Reporting Initiative Status Report* (Washington D.C.: February 2010).

[18] GAO, *Internal Control: Standards for Internal Control in the Federal Government*, GAO/AIMD-00-21.3.1 (Washington, D.C.: November 1999).

[19] Officials from one of the two remaining JTTFs said they did not know if the NSI process was working well, and officials from the other JTTF said the NSI process was not working well because they were not aware of it. We interviewed both line officers and analysts from the Federal Protective Service and the Bureau of Alcohol, Tobacco, Firearms and Explosives. One bureau analyst we met with did not know if the process was working well. One Federal Protective Service line officer said that the process is not working well because law enforcement officials had multiple ways to report SARs.

[20] FBI investigative criteria are documented in its *Domestic Investigations and Operations Guide*.

[21] Officials from the other three JTTFs we met with did not raise this concern.

[22] The fusion centers that said they conducted investigative work were not always in the same jurisdictions as the JTTFs that raised concerns about such actions.

[23] To participate in the NSI, fusion centers are required to have access to eGuardian and the NSI Federated Search. Having access to eGuardian enables them to submit ISE- SARs to, and review and analyze ISE-SARs within, eGuardian. Having access to the NSI Federated Search enables them to review and analyze ISE-SARs in Shared Spaces. Many fusion centers have also chosen to obtain a Shared Spaces server, which enables them to contribute ISE-SARs to Shared Spaces.

[24] We discuss the automatic sharing of ISE-SARs between Shared Spaces and eGuardian later in this report.

[25] Costs associated with Guardian are available on the federal information technology (IT) Dashboard—a website that enables the general public and other stakeholders to view details of federal IT investments.

[26] The ISA IPC—within the Executive Office of the President—has a SAR Subcommittee that is responsible for resolving related interagency disputes, among other things.

[27] The FBI has access to ISE-SARs in Shared Spaces through the Federated Search, but FBI headquarters officials said that it is difficult to systematically try to match ISE-SARs in eGuardian to the ISE-SARs in Shared Spaces because Shared Spaces does not allow users to search for ISE-SARs that were entered during a specific time frame.

[28] The Associate Attorney General advises and assists the Attorney General and the Deputy Attorney General in formulating and implementing departmental policies and programs.

[29] Correspondence to address the FBI's concerns included a message to fusion centers and other NSI stakeholders entitled, PMO, *A Call to Action: A Unified Message Regarding the Need to Support Suspicious Activity Reporting and Training* (April 2012).

[30] DOJ's written comments are reproduced in appendix VII.

[31] The Privacy Officer at a fourth fusion center said that his center was using Shared Spaces only to submit ISE-SARs at the time of our interviews. Subsequently, the official said the center received a legal opinion from the State Police that allows the center to simultaneously submit ISE-SARs to both systems.

[32] In commenting on a draft of this report, FBI officials noted that in February 2013, the FBI implemented a new feature in eGuardian that allows fusion centers to directly and electronically remove their ISE-SARs. ISE-SARs that are removed from eGuardian are still retained in Guardian and other FBI systems in accordance with their retention schedules. See appendix V for eGuardian and Guardian retention schedules.

[33] All SARs submitted to eGuardian are automatically sent to Guardian, which operates under different retention policies. See appendix V for eGuardian and Guardian SAR retention schedules.

[34] See, e.g., 28 C.F.R. §23.20(h) (providing that information contained in a criminal intelligence system operating through support under the Omnibus Crime Control and Safe Streets act of 1968, as amended, shall not be retained for longer than 5 years).

[35] See, for example, DOJ, *The Department of Justice Systems Development Life Cycle Guidance Document*.

[36] According to PMO and FBI officials, ISE-SARs are transmitted from an entity's local system to its Shared Spaces server, and then from its Shared Spaces server to eGuardian. The first interconnection—the initial push of ISE-SARs from a fusion center's local system to its Shared Spaces server—was beyond the scope of our review, but could still affect the quality of the data received by NSI stakeholders and would need to be factored into plans for performing interoperability measures going forward.

[37] The PMO later indicated that it had followed DOJ's *Systems Development Life Cycle Guidance*, but they were unable to provide any of the documentation that would necessarily result from doing so.

[38] Line officers are law enforcement officers whose routine duties put them in a position to observe suspicious activity. Analytical personnel are officials from fusion centers and federal agencies that may have responsibilities to review SARs to determine if they have a nexus to terrorism. Executives are senior fusion center officials that are responsible for determining whether their fusion centers will participate in the NSI.

[39] Our work focused on executive, analyst, and line officer training that had been developed and rolled out to stakeholders for several years. Our work did not include the implementation of training to the private sector and homeland security partners that was just made available to stakeholders in April 2012.

[40] The number of respondents differs because not all of those who took the survey answered all questions.

[41] GAO

[42] See appendix II for additional information on the behaviors associated with each category of suspicious activity.

[43] According to FBI officials, the FBI reviews all SARs to determine if additional actions should be taken, such as a threat assessment or investigation. SARs that do not initially lead to an investigation may still have analytical value or provide useful information to help identify trends or provide context to other reported incidents.

[44] DHS I&A, *Survey of Analytic Production Incorporating Suspicious Activity Reporting* (Washington, D.C.: 2011).

[45] PM-ISE, *Nationwide Suspicious Activity Reporting Initiative Status Report*, (Washington, D.C.: February 2010).

[46] See, for example, GAO, *Information Sharing: DHS Could Better Define How It Plans to Meet Its State and Local Mission and Improve Performance Accountability*, GAO-11-223 (Washington D.C.: Dec. 16, 2010), and *Aviation Security: A National Strategy and Other Actions Would Strengthen TSA's Efforts to Secure Commercial Airport Perimeters and Access Controls*, GAO-09-399 (Washington, D.C.: Sept. 30, 2009).

[47] GAO, *Supply Chain Security: CBP Needs to Conduct Regular Assessments of Its Cargo Targeting System*, GAO-13-9 (Washington, D.C.: Oct. 25, 2012).

[48] Project Management Institute, *The Standard for Program Management* ©.

[49] The PM-ISE plans for, oversees implementation of, and manages the government-wide Information Sharing Environment (ISE)—an approach for sharing terrorism-related information that may include any method deemed necessary and appropriate. See 6 U.S.C. § 485(a)(3), (f).

[50] Unlike a random sample, a nonprobability sample is more deliberatively chosen, meaning that some elements of the population being studied have either no chance or an unknown chance of being selected as part of the sample.

[51] In general, the E-Government Act of 2002 mandates that federal agencies conduct privacy impact assessments to ensure sufficient protections for the privacy of personal information

that may be collected, maintained, or disseminated using information technology. See Pub. L. No. 107-347, § 208, 116 Stat. 2899, 2921-23 (2002).

[52] See, DOJ, *The Department of Justice Systems Development Life Cycle Guidance Document* (Washington D.C.: January 2003).

[53] See, for example, GAO, *Human Capital: A Guide for Assessing Strategic Training and Development Efforts in the Federal Government*, GAO-04-546G (Washington D.C.: March 2004).

[54] The Project Management Institute, *The Standard for Program Management* ©.

[55] The federal agencies participating in the NSI include independent federal agencies and government corporations. FBI officials did not provide a complete listing of participating DOD agencies. They explained that DOD is responsible for implementing the NSI within the department.

In: Nationwide Suspicious Activity …
Editor: Laurits Hartmann
ISBN: 978-1-62618-766-5
© 2013 Nova Science Publishers, Inc.

Chapter 3

NATIONWIDE SAR INITIATIVE: ANNUAL REPORT 2011*

U.S. Department of Justice

EXECUTIVE BRIEFING

The Nationwide Suspicious Activity Reporting (SAR) Initiative (NSI) Program Management Office (PMO) was established in March 2010 and is a collaborative effort led by the U.S. Department of Justice (DOJ), Bureau of Justice Assistance (BJA), in partnership with the U.S. Department of Homeland Security (DHS), the Federal Bureau of Investigation (FBI), and state, local, tribal, and territorial (SLTT) law enforcement partners. The NSI PMO has been working with the National Network of Fusion Centers, hometown security partners, and SLTT and federal law enforcement to implement the policies, processes, and standards of the NSI across all levels of government while ensuring that privacy, civil rights, and civil liberties are protected.

Over the past year, the NSI PMO has brought in new staff members who have become essential in the continued development of the NSI. The addition of the Executive Support Specialists provides law enforcement and NSI experts to the field, so they can help NSI sites with training, technical assistance, policy development and guidance, and outreach to key stakeholders

* This is an edited, reformatted and augmented version of the Bureau of Justice Assistance, U.S. department of Justice, dated 2011.

and chief executives, while also ensuring that NSI sites have met all of the requirements for implementation. The NSI has worked diligently in implementing the standards, policies, and processes of the NSI across the National Network of Fusion Centers, and as of March 2012, 68 fusion centers have the capability to contribute and share suspicious activity reports, expanding the reach of the NSI to over 14,000 law enforcement agencies in 46 states, including the District of Columbia. The expansion of the NSI has allowed the Federated Search Tool to be accessed by more trained users—increasing the number of searches to more than 43,000— and over 17,000 SARs were submitted for sharing by the end of March 2011.

Since the inception of the NSI, the FBI has been a vital partner in the success of sharing terrorism-related information. Over the past year, the FBI's eGuardian team has worked closely with the NSI PMO to address and finalize issues with system compatibility, data synchronization, and alignment of policies. Through their commitment to work together, the NSI PMO and the FBI conducted outreach to the National Network of Fusion Centers to ensure that NSI sites understand the SAR reporting process, as well as the full integration of the eGuardian system and how this will help continue to improve the sharing of suspicious activity.

Launched in conjunction with the NSI, the DHS "If You See Something, Say Something™" campaign made major strides over the past year in raising public awareness of indicators related to terrorism and encouraging individuals to report suspicious activity to their local law enforcement authorities. Also, to help support the efforts of the NSI PMO, the DHS Office of Intelligence and Analysis began working to establish baseline metrics and to evaluate the analytic value of SAR information submitted to the NSI Federated Search. This will help provide support for requests for information across the divisions, as well as external state and local support requests (SLSRs), NSI-derived production of Roll Call Releases, and support to other products.

The NSI PMO has maintained a focus on reaching out to key stakeholders across the country, informing them of updates and advances to current NSI programs and training initiatives, as well as technology improvements. In the past year, the NSI Line Officer Training has been delivered to agencies and associations all over the country, and with their effort, approximately 250,000 frontline officers have reported receiving the training. With the success of the NSI Line Officer Training, the next task the NSI took on was to produce a SAR awareness training program for partners with similar missions to those of law enforcement constituencies, also referred to as hometown security partners, on behaviors and indicators of terrorist-related activity that they may come across while performing their daily responsibilities. The NSI PMO, with the assistance of subject-matter experts, developed sector-specific training for fire service and emergency medical services personnel, public safety telecommunications professionals (e.g., 9-1-1 operators), emergency managers, corrections and probation and parole officers, and private sector security personnel and those charged with protecting the nation's critical infrastructure.

Along with the development of the SAR Hometown Security Partners Training, the NSI PMO has continued to work with local law enforcement agencies on building relationships with community leaders through the Building Communities of Trust (BCOT) initiative. This initiative focuses on developing trust among law enforcement, fusion centers, and the communities they serve, particularly immigrant and minority communities, so that crime and terrorism can be addressed. The newly published *Building Communities of Trust: A Guidance for Community Leaders* was developed in partnership with DOJ, DHS, and the International Association of Chiefs of Police (IACP) to assist community leaders in working with law enforcement agencies to facilitate dialogue and discuss ways to work together to prevent crime and terrorism.

In addition to outreach to stakeholders and the community, over the past year the NSI PMO worked with the Office of the Program Manager, Information Sharing Environment (PM-ISE); the FBI; IACP— specifically the IACP Homeland Security and Terrorism Committees—and many other key federal, state, and local representatives and law enforcement associations to develop a Unified Message that reinforces the importance of SLTT and federal entities working together to fight terrorism and help keep our communities safe. This document reiterates the importance of suspicious activity reporting and training frontline law enforcement officers so they know what behaviors and indicators to look for while still ensuring privacy, civil rights, and civil liberties protections when they do. This message also underscores the importance of the sharing of SAR information with the FBI's Joint Terrorism Task Forces (JTTFs) for further investigation and with state and major urban area fusion centers (fusion centers) for analysis. The Unified Message also reinforces the important role local communities play and encourages them to work together with DHS on the "If You See Something, Say Something™" campaign, which raises public awareness of behavioral indicators of terrorism and emphasizes the importance of the public in reporting suspicious activities to local law enforcement.

Over the past year, the NSI PMO made a number of technology improvements to the NSI Federated Search and has also provided resources to assist users, if needed. These new modifications include a Single Line Search, similar to a Google search; a subscription service, where users can create and save queries; a new NSI Analytical Tool that will allow users to review specific information easily; and also a Help Desk and Frequently Asked Questions (FAQs) site, where users will find useful information pertaining to the NSI program.

Update on the Nationwide SAR Initiative

NSI Program Management Office (PMO)

The NSI PMO welcomed aboard new staff members during the past year: in March 2011, the FBI detailed a new Deputy Director, and in November 2011, the DHS detailed a new Principal Deputy Director. The NSI PMO also welcomed four Executive Support Specialists to the team this year. This team of highly qualified state and local law enforcement leaders is charged with providing hands-on technical assistance to NSI sites within their specific region and ensuring that those sites have met all of the requirements for NSI implementation. This includes scheduling needed training; providing executive briefings, policy development, and guidance; and educating sites on technical updates to the Federated Search. In addition, the Executive Support Specialists are able to help sites strategize on deployment of the frontline officer training, which is a critical component of the NSI process.

Implementation

The NSI PMO staff worked diligently over the past 12 months to implement the standards, policies, and processes of the NSI across the National Network of Fusion Centers. As of March 2012, 68 fusion centers had the capability to contribute and share suspicious activity reports, as well as DHS, the FBI, and Amtrak. Outreach efforts are under way to implement the final participating fusion centers, which include fusion centers that were just stood up in 2011, into the NSI process. The expected completion of this is September 2012.

The NSI, through the National Network of Fusion Centers, now reaches over 14,000 law enforcement agencies in 46 states and the District of Columbia.

Utilization

As the NSI has expanded to more sites, there has been a commensurate increase in users and utilization of the NSI Federated Search. As of March 2012, more than 43,000 searches had been conducted and over 17,000 SAR reports were available for analysts to search in the system. Maturity of the NSI has served as a strong enabler for fusion centers in developing relevant products that advance the situational awareness of their mutual stakeholders. Fusion centers are uniquely situated to provide an analytic context to SAR data, an essential element of the NSI's overall mission.

Incorporation of eGuardian

eGuardian has been a partner with the NSI ever since the NSI's official inception in 2010. As such, the FBI has worked continually with the NSI in order to ensure that eGuardian and the NSI's Federated Search complement each other to achieve a shared mission of preventing terrorism by effectively sharing SAR data. Continued improvements over the past year have addressed system compatibility, record retention policies, data collection synchronization, and unified outreach to fusion centers regarding SAR reporting. The FBI's classified Guardian system (to which eGuardian migrates suspicious activity reports for investigative follow-up) has administered record retention policies that closely mirror those of 28 CFR Part 23, the federal regulation that governs how law enforcement agencies operate criminal intelligence information systems while properly protecting individuals' privacy, civil rights, and civil liberties. In addition, the NSI has taken steps to facilitate the automated migration of SAR entries from the Federated Search to eGuardian in order to ensure that they are received by a JTTF. The FBI, the NSI, and DHS have also worked to foster a unified approach towards educating fusion centers on the changes that have taken place with respect to the SAR reporting process. Through a commitment by both the FBI and the NSI to ensure the integration of eGuardian and the Federated Search, similar improvements and enhancements will continue to be implemented to ensure the seamless sharing of terrorism-related information. The value of JTTFs in receiving SAR data is exemplified by the fact that over 700 terrorism investigations have been initiated by the FBI based on information received from eGuardian (April 2012).

An eGuardian incident was entered by FBI Headquarters (FBI HQ) personnel after an Internet tip from the Philippines claiming a named crew member of a privately owned cruise ship was intentionally infecting Americans with the AIDS virus. The subject was also about to place an explosive device on the ship with the intention of killing Americans. FBI HQ personnel were able to determine that the corporate headquarters for the cruise line was in Seattle, Washington. The incident was being prepared for transfer within the Guardian system to the Seattle Division. The legitimacy of the information was not known, nor was the name or whereabouts of the ship to which the subject crew member was supposedly assigned. Within minutes after placing the unclassified information into eGuardian, a telephone call came to FBI HQ from an analyst at the Pacific Regional Information Clearinghouse (PacClear). The analyst had an eGuardian account and noticed this new incident, which listed the contact number for the person who created it. The analyst was able to verify that a person with the same name as the subject had entered the United States from the Philippines on an employment visa and was in fact an employee of the named cruise line. Further, the analyst advised that the subject was assigned to a ship that was currently docked in Miami. This example of information sharing allowed FBI HQ to immediately forward the time-sensitive incident, via Guardian, to the Miami JTTF instead of the Seattle JTTF. The Miami JTTF was able to quickly locate both the ship and the subject. It was determined that the subject had sent e-mails indicating an intention to carry out a terrorist act; however, no explosives were found, and the pending threat was immediately mitigated. The collaboration between eGuardian and Guardian and between the fusion center and the FBI JTTF allowed for a quick response by law enforcement. Had this been a legitimate threat, this act of terrorism would have been prevented.

Expanded Efforts

Gang Data Exchange Standard Pilot Implementation

This initiative builds on the work of the Global Justice Information Sharing Initiative's (Global) Intelligence Working Group's (GIWG) Gang

Intelligence Strategy Committee (GISC) and the Criminal Intelligence Coordinating Council's (CICC) efforts to improve and enhance national capabilities to share gang data. The first step completed was the development of the Gang Information Exchange Packet Document (IEPD), which identifies the data elements to be shared in a national Federated Search, as well as to identify statewide gang initiatives for use in a pilot project. The goal of the project is to have the National Gang Federated Search Tool located on the National Gang Intelligence Center (NGIC) Web site, within a secure environment, which will be accessible through both the FBI's Law Enforcement Online (LEO) and the Regional Information Sharing Systems® (RISS). Another aspect of the project is to look at the gang data elements in the FBI's Violent Gang and Terrorist Organization File (VGTOF) and determine whether it is possible to conduct an electronic push of data from local gang systems in the future. The project will also look at utilizing VGTOF as a data source in the Federated Search.

This initiative was developed based on the lessons learned of the NSI, including the segment and solution architecture and the technological relationship with fusion centers, as well as how to facilitate the sharing of information in a secure manner while providing an economic solution that maintains local control.

Terrorist Screening Center

The Terrorist Screening Center (TSC) is the agency responsible for maintaining the U.S. government's consolidated Terrorist Watchlist, which is a single database of identifying information about people who are known or reasonably suspected of being involved in terrorist activity. Over the past several months, the TSC and the NSI PMO entered into discussions about providing an electronic notification to the fusion centers and notifying multiple fusion centers as needed. The TSC is currently working to develop an electronic bulletin board on a secure but unclassified (SBU) system to post timely TSC encounter information and is also developing an immediate notification mechanism that simultaneously sends e-mail alerts to fusion centers.

ISA IPC SAR Sub-Committee

The Information Sharing and Access (ISA) Interagency Policy Committee (IPC) Suspicious Activity Reporting (SAR) Sub-Committee is a results-oriented body responsible for providing the ISA IPC policy recommendations for gathering, analyzing, and sharing SAR information across levels of government, the private sector, and mission areas. The SAR Sub-Committee's focus is on broader policies for SAR information sharing, as opposed to the NSI, which is focused on implementation of the standardized process for gathering, analyzing, and sharing terrorism-related SAR information.

In 2011, the SAR Sub-Committee met six times, focusing on expanding support to SAR at the federal level through policy and guidance, as well as recommending priorities for evolution of the NSI. This included the development of best practices for analysts in the field to fully utilize SAR information, developing a Concept of Operations for SAR analysis at the federal level, and determining next steps for using the NSI model for a larger priority crimes platform.

UNIFIED MESSAGE

The attacks of 9/11 and the current dynamic threat environment demonstrate that no single organization can address terrorism alone. Every agency connected to the NSI mission, from the federal government to local police and sheriff's departments, must work together to share information that may prevent the next attack. Until recently, the federal government did not always provide clear, consistent guidance to SLTT and private sector partners on how and where to share information relating to suspicious activity. To help clarify the message and enhance existing partnerships and information sharing, the IACP hosted a series of meetings with very senior representatives from state, local, and federal agencies, as well as law enforcement associations and other stakeholders, to create a unified approach to the reporting and sharing of information related to suspicious activity.

As a result of these meetings and coordination, there is now broad consensus on the message among law enforcement, homeland security agencies, and associations. A Unified Message document was created that provides clear guidance to the public that they should report any suspicious activity to law enforcement. The Unified Message encourages agencies at all levels—state, local, tribal, and territorial—to work with DHS on its "If You See Something, Say Something™" campaign to raise public awareness of behavioral indicators of terrorism and to emphasize the importance of the public in reporting suspicious activities to the proper law enforcement authorities, who will forward suspicious activity reports to the FBI's JTTFs for further investigation and to fusion centers for analysis.

> Efforts to address crime and threats in our communities are most effective when they involve strong collaboration between law enforcement and the communities and citizens they serve. Law enforcement and homeland security professionals are responsible for ensuring that the public understands how to report suspicious activity and that agency/organizational members support the collection, analysis, and submission of suspicious activity reports to the proper fusion center or FBI JTTF.

The Unified Message also reinforces the importance of frontline officer training on identifying and reporting those behaviors and activities that are potentially indicative of terrorist or other criminal activity and provides direction to agencies on preparing SARs and how to ensure the protection of privacy, civil rights, and civil liberties when doing so. The Unified Message calls on law enforcement executives to conduct SAR training within their agencies and provides online resources for their use. The NSI PMO and the FBI worked closely together to ensure the interoperability between two systems: eGuardian and the Shared Space. Whether personnel enter a SAR into the eGuardian system or the Shared Space system, the other system will receive it.

> On July 12, 2011, at approximately 17:00 hours, two U.S. military personnel, one in U.S. Marine Corps (USMC) uniform and the other in civilian attire, were traveling northbound on Interstate 5 in Seattle, Washington, in a government-licensed vehicle after leaving the Seattle Military Entrance Processing Station (MEPS). A blue Geo Metro vehicle, with Washington plates pulled up beside them and then braked in order to get behind them. The male driver of the Geo Metro (later identified as Mr. Michael McCright) appeared to look at the government license plate, then sped up to pull abreast of their vehicle.
>
> After a few seconds, Mr. McCright suddenly swerved his vehicle at the government vehicle in an attempt to run it off the freeway. The Marines pulled off the freeway and called 9-1-1 to report the incident.
>
> After returning to the Marine Corps Recruitment Office, the Marines also reported the incident to their Commanding Officer.

The information was then passed to the Antiterrorism (AT) Officer for the 12th Marine Recruiting District, in San Diego, California. The AT Officer then initiated a Tip and Lead (T&L) report, which was ultimately forwarded to the Washington State Fusion Center (WSFC) as a result of the officer's past interactions with a fusion center in California. Once the T&L arrived in the WSFC's Intake e- mail, it was reviewed by an intake analyst for processing. The intake process identified inconsistencies in Mr. McCright's activities and necessitated further vetting and investigation of the situation with more thorough background checks and case preparation. Simultaneously, a suspicious activity report (SAR) was entered into the Nationwide SAR Initiative (NSI) database, and the case was assigned to a fusion center detective for investigative follow-up.

A Washington State Patrol (WSP) detective currently assigned to the WSFC coordinated the case with the Seattle Division Joint Terrorism Task Force, which corresponded with an existing FBI investigation. The joint investigation quickly unveiled the severity of Mr. McCright's motives when it was discovered that he had recently been in cell phone contact with Mr. Abu Khalid Abdul-Latif, who was charged in the recently foiled Seattle terrorism plot in June 2011. Mr. Abdul-Latif, of Seattle, and Mr. Walli Mujahidh, of Los Angeles, California, were charged with plotting to attack the Seattle MEPS with small-arms fire and grenades. Contact or communication with known or suspected terrorists is viewed by the Intelligence Community as an observable violent or criminal radicalization behavior. Based on the investigation, an arrest warrant was obtained. Mr. McCright was arrested on September 8, 2011, on two counts of assault in the second degree. The arrest was conducted to ensure that Mr. McCright would be in custody prior to the weekend of the ten-year anniversary of the September 11, 2001, attacks, and because of his ties to a known terror suspect, his bail was set for $2 million. Further investigation was conducted regarding his possible ties to other violent extremists and possible involvement in suspicious surveillance of a military recruiting center.

The process—from reporting the suspicious activity to the investigation and through to the arrest—was successful due to the emphasis placed on reporting suspicious activities to the appropriate law enforcement authorities and the deep collaboration among the WSP, the Seattle Police Department, the FBI, and the WSFC.

The constantly evolving national security threat requires an adaptable information sharing strategy. The NSI PMO is committed to the timely sharing of intelligence and will continue to work with federal, SLTT, and private sector partners to implement and mature the NSI.

The complete document, *A Call to Action: A Unified Message Regarding the Need to Support Suspicious Activity Reporting and Training*, is located in Appendix 3.

STAKEHOLDER AND COMMUNITY ENGAGEMENT

Speaking Engagements

The NSI PMO has made it a priority to reach out to key stakeholders, informing them of current activities as well as future plans and developments within the NSI program. Over the past year, NSI PMO representatives participated in more than 80 conferences and executive-level meetings, cutting across law enforcement; private industry; emergency management; fire and EMS services; corrections, probation, and parole; and critical infrastructure and key resources sectors. This outreach has helped inform the development of training and has been critical to ensuring that stakeholders understand the standards, policies, and processes of the NSI as they are being implemented and as the program matures beyond providing the capabilities and into the utilization of those capabilities by those in the field.

NSI User/Analyst Meetings

In February 2011, the NSI PMO began hosting semiannual invitation-only Analyst User Meetings. These meetings are designed to highlight technological/system enhancements, engage in candid discussion on the use of the NSI Federated Search and eGuardian, identify SAR analysis best practices, resolve common debates regarding the vetting process, and make suggestions for additional training for analysts. Two of these meetings were held in the past year, and fusion centers were asked to identify analysts or other personnel from their fusion center who are the most familiar with vetting and analysis of SAR data and routinely utilize the NSI Federated Search. These regular, in-person feedback sessions are designed to improve the processes of the NSI and ensure that the technical functions of the Federated Search meet the needs of the field, as well as help shape future select policy issues as the NSI matures.

Building Communities of Trust: A Guidance for Community Leaders and Program Update

The Building Communities of Trust (BCOT) initiative focuses on developing trust among law enforcement, fusion centers, and the communities they serve, particularly immigrant and minority communities, so that crime and terrorism can be addressed. This initiative has been administered primarily by the NSI, a program that provides law enforcement with a capacity for gathering, documenting, processing, analyzing, and sharing suspicious activity reports about behaviors that have a potential nexus to terrorism. The NSI recognizes that each community has one of the most important roles in the prevention of crime and terrorism, since law enforcement agencies are dependent on community members to report suspicious activity information to SLTT law enforcement officers. To help ensure that this reporting takes place, it is essential that law enforcement and community members have strong, trusting relationships. As these relationships are developed and maintained, members of the community are more likely to report crime and suspicious activities, which is why the NSI has worked with partners at the federal, state, and local levels—including U.S. Attorneys' Offices, privacy advocacy groups, faith leaders, and a diverse group of local community members—to implement the BCOT initiative.

Over the past year, the NSI, in coordination with DHS and the IACP, worked with local law enforcement agencies across the country to host Building Communities of Trust roundtables. The purpose of these meetings was to help open dialogue between law enforcement and community leaders, as well as to inform about the development of a new product, *Building Communities of Trust: A Guidance for Community Leaders*. This document provides recommendations, resources, and tips on proactively working with law enforcement agencies to keep neighborhoods safe.

The BCOT initiative was also highlighted as a best practice in the White House Strategy "Empowering Local Partners to Prevent Violent Extremism in the United States" and subsequent Strategic Implementation Plan. The BCOT initiative was also featured in the Countering Violent Extremism (CVE) Workshop sponsored by DHS in Columbus, Ohio, in August 2011.

BCOT partnered with the IACP and DHS this year by holding meetings in several major urban areas, including San Francisco, California; San Jose, California; Oakland, California; and Aurora, Colorado. Because of the previous successes with roundtables held in 2010, follow-up sessions were also held in Chicago, Illinois, and Seattle, Washington, at the request of the law enforcement agencies and in coordination with the local U.S. Attorneys' Offices.

"If You See Something, Say Something™"

The DHS "If You See Something, Say Something™" campaign, a public awareness and engagement initiative encouraging public reporting of suspicious activity to local law enforcement, has continued to grow since its initial launch in July 2010.

The campaign was originally used by New York's Metropolitan Transportation Authority (MTA), which licensed the use of the slogan to DHS for anti-terrorism and anti-terrorism crime-related efforts. The "If You See Something, Say Something™" campaign is being launched in conjunction with the rollout of the NSI.

A critical element of the DHS mission is ensuring that the civil rights and civil liberties of persons are not diminished by our security efforts, activities, and programs. The "If You See Something, Say Something™" campaign focuses on behaviors and indicators, rather than appearance, in identifying suspicious activity.

Factors such as race, ethnicity, national origin, or religious affiliation alone are not suspicious. For that reason, the public should report only suspicious behavior and activities (e.g., an unattended backpack in a public place or someone trying to break into a restricted area) rather than beliefs, thoughts, ideas, expressions, associations, or speech unrelated to terrorism or other criminal activity. Only reports that document behavior reasonably indicative of criminal activity related to terrorism will be shared with federal partners.

Partnerships include a variety of cities and states, universities, private companies, and all of the major sports leagues, including Major League Baseball, Major League Soccer, the National Basketball Association, the National Football League, the National Hockey League, the U.S. Open—Golf and Tennis, and IndyCar and NASCAR, as well as Minor League Baseball. DHS will continue to work to expand the initiative in the coming months.

A California motorist noticed a very muddy vehicle traveling on a highway near Los Angeles. As the motorist passed the vehicle, he noticed two occupants—a male driver and a female passenger—who were videotaping themselves. The female passenger appeared to be holding a device with wires coming out of it. When the driver in the muddy vehicle became aware that the other motorist had noticed them, he pulled a mask down over his face and sped away. The motorist was able to obtain the vehicle registration plate and reported the incident to local police, who checked the residence of the registered owner but were unable to locate him or the vehicle. The report was also placed into eGuardian by the local police agency. The local JTTF immediately received the incident after the transfer from eGuardian to Guardian and began checking internal FBI databases, as well as other publicly available sources. The JTTF determined that a telephone number of the suspicious vehicle owner had been in contact with a telephone number belonging to other persons under indictment in Washington State for terrorist acts, including a plot to kill U.S. government employees and police officers. Had this information not been effectively shared with the FBI, where internal systems could be cross-referenced, the associated telephone numbers would likely have never been discovered. As a result of this suspicious information, which was provided by a local police agency utilizing eGuardian, nefarious associations were found and a new terrorism investigation was initiated.

International Association of Chiefs of Police Information Sharing 101 Training

The continued partnership of the NSI PMO with the IACP was strengthened over the past year with the inclusion of SAR principles and practices within the recently released curriculum supporting the State, Local, and Tribal (SLT) Domestic Security project, also known as SLT101. Through this project, the IACP has developed a curriculum designed specifically to address the growing demands of SLT agencies to better participate in the Information Sharing Environment (ISE). This training includes a seminar and online tutorials and will provide attendees with a resource tool kit to help guide the process.

The purpose of this training is to increase the knowledge of law enforcement executives of the various aspects of the ISE and to close the information gaps that may exist. Additionally, this training is designed to promote information sharing and analysis for the purpose of safeguarding communities in the United States while protecting the privacy, civil rights, and civil liberties of citizens. Special emphasis was given to the NSI, implementation of Fusion Liaison Officer (FLO) or Terrorism Liaison Officer (TLO) programs, and increased interaction and connectivity with fusion centers.

This training was held in ten locations across the country, reaching approximately 300 chief executives and other law enforcement partners.

PRIVACY

As of March 2012, the National Network of Fusion Centers consisted of 77 primary and recognized fusion centers, as designated by state governors. By the end of March 2012, all of these fusion centers had developed privacy policies determined to be at least as comprehensive as the ISE Privacy Guidelines. The NSI PMO continues to work with fusion centers to implement the standards, policies, and processes of the NSI, so that they can share terrorism-related SARs with other participating NSI locations.

The CICC developed the *Privacy, Civil Rights, and Civil Liberties Compliance Verification for the Intelligence Enterprise* resource to assist agencies as they review and assess their policies and procedures related to privacy, civil rights, and civil liberties protections to ensure these policies are comprehensive and have been fully implemented. The template is recommended for use as a self- assessment tool within a law enforcement agency and is being used to promote peer-to-peer exchanges between similar intelligence enterprises. This peer-to-peer process will increase communication and coordination between agencies, identify smart practices, and provide feedback and recommendations to mitigate potential implementation gaps. In early 2010, the template was successfully piloted through a peer-to-peer exchange by the joint DHS/DOJ Fusion Process Technical Assistance Program between the Georgia Information Sharing and Analysis Center and the Florida Fusion Center.

Following this initial pilot and the development of the SAR Appendix, the NSI PMO, in collaboration with the DHS/DOJ Fusion Process Technical Assistance Program, offered the primary and designated fusion centers to undergo a peer-to-peer exchange to implement the *Privacy, Civil Rights, and Civil Liberties Compliance Verification for the Intelligence Enterprise*.

TRAINING

The NSI training strategy is a multifaceted approach designed to increase the effectiveness of SLTT law enforcement and public safety professionals and other frontline partners in identifying, reporting, evaluating, and sharing pre-incident terrorism indicators to prevent acts of terrorism. The overarching goal of the training strategy is to facilitate appropriate agency implementation of the SAR process and to enhance a nationwide SAR capability. To achieve this goal, the NSI has developed and deployed training programs for frontline officers, analysts, chief executives, and hometown security partners regarding the behaviors and indicators of terrorism-related criminal activity.

> State and local law enforcement agencies in Arizona and Georgia have worked to cultivate relationships with the Peace Officer Standards and Training (POST) associations to advance the SAR training message through the state POST requirements process.

Hometown Security Partners

While continuing to provide high-quality training for the law enforcement community, the NSI has developed SAR awareness training for hometown security partners that are important to the SAR effort, including fire and emergency medical services personnel, public safety telecommunications professionals (e.g., 9-1-1 operators), emergency managers, corrections and probation and parole officers, and private sector security personnel and those charged with protecting the nation's critical infrastructure. The purpose is not to empower public safety officials to act on behalf of law enforcement but to have them understand the critical role they play in identifying and reporting suspicious activity to SLTT law enforcement.

9-1-1 is the number most people in the United States call to obtain help in a police, fire, or medical emergency, which uniquely affords 9-1-1 call-takers the opportunity to play an important role in SAR awareness. The responsibilities of the emergency management community include working closely with operators and owners of critical infrastructure and key resources, responding to emergency situations, and gathering information about disasters, which may place them in unique positions to observe suspicious activity-related behaviors and indicators that, when viewed within the totality of circumstances, may indicate preoperational planning of a terrorist-related incident. Firefighters also have a significant reach into communities across America. In their efforts to prevent and respond to life and property losses, firefighters enter homes, businesses, vehicles, and other assets thousands of times each day and, as a result, may encounter behaviors and/or indicators of criminal activity. Community corrections professionals are also in a position to recognize criminal or potential terrorism activity, especially while this activity may be in the planning phase, due to their contact with offenders and families and friends of offenders. With more than 2 million security officers who protect our nation's critical infrastructure, these public safety and security professionals can be "force multipliers" to help recognize and report suspicious activity.

In order to ensure that this training was relevant for each of these specific sectors, the NSI PMO conducted a two-day focus group session consisting of subject-matter experts from these fields. The input provided by these experts was critical to the development of the training and will be an important factor in the rollout, which began in spring 2012. In particular, there were several associations that partnered with the NSI PMO, including:

- International Association of Fire Chiefs
- Association of Public-Safety Communications Officials
- National Emergency Management Association
- American Probation and Parole Association
- ASIS International
- National Association of Security Companies

The support and partnership from these associations is necessary for the success of the training package, and the NSI PMO will work with each of them over the coming year to help ensure that the training is pushed out to the memberships of each of these sectors.

National Maritime Intelligence-Integration Office

The National Maritime Intelligence-Integration Office (NMIO), in partnership with the NSI PMO, is bringing a SAR awareness training program that will focus on the maritime industry and the many individuals connected to port facilities. The purpose is not to empower port and private safety officials to act on behalf of law enforcement but to have them understand the critical role they play in identifying and reporting suspicious activity to SLTT law enforcement.

The United States conducts 95 percent of commercial trade via maritime conveyances—moving over 2 billion tons of freight a year and handling $264 billion in annual commerce. The U.S. maritime responsibility includes 164,000 employees in water transportation and ports, 200,000 foreign sailors, 7 million cruise passengers, and 134 million ferry passengers. Including the management of the security of the coastlines means there are over 25,000 miles of inland waterways, 95,000 miles of shoreline, 240- plus shipyards, and 1,000 harbor channels that need to be monitored.

NMIO and the NSI PMO plan to complete the development of the maritime industry sector training by the fall of 2012. The delivery of the new training module will be similar in format to other SAR Hometown Security Partners Training and will be accessed via familiar training portals and hard-copy CDs or DVDs. Additionally, the NSI PMO and NMIO are partnering with DHS, the United States Coast Guard, and the U.S. Department of Transportation's Maritime Administration (MARAD) to provide specialized presentations and discussions at ten ports across the nation. The intended outcome of these visits is to enhance the SAR business processes and ultimately capture a business process/model that can be replicated across the nation's ports. The training and port visits will serve to educate those professions within the maritime industry who have the best potential of being exposed to harbor- related indicators and behaviors associated with criminal and/or terrorist activity.

NSI Analyst Technical Assistance

Contributing SAR information to the NSI Federated Search is only the first step to leveraging the value of the NSI Federated Search. The next step relates to the fusion center analysts' ability to search the shared information as part of the analytical process and to receive valuable information. To enhance this process, the NSI has developed an NSI Federated Search Tool Technical Assistance process for fusion center analysts. This technical assistance process provides analysts with the capability to quickly and effectively search for relevant information within the NSI Federated Search. This assistance will be primarily provided by the NSI Executive Support Specialists. The technical assistance offering lasts approximately four hours and will demonstrate how users can access the NSI Federated Search Tool via RISS and/or LEO and how to use the NSI Federated Search Tool. The technical assistance offering provides a live, thorough overview of the two primary search methods: the Single Line Search and the Advanced Search. It also includes an overview of the State and Local Anti-Terrorism Training (SLATT®) Database Search and the User Toolbar. Analysts will learn how to display the data in a geospatial format using the Map It/Link It tool. In addition to searching and mapping the data, the analysts will also learn how to save queries, set alert notifications, and locate contact information.

SAR Analyst Training

Over the past year, the NSI PMO worked to deliver 24 analyst training sessions across the country, reaching almost 700 analysts. In addition, upon receiving authorization from the NSI PMO to conduct in- house SAR Analyst Training, DHS conducted three deliveries of the training in 2011. These sessions were well attended by personnel from nine DHS components, with a total of 83 people trained.

Line Officer Training Update

The NSI PMO continued to make great strides in providing SAR training to law enforcement and support personnel to help ensure that they are trained to recognize behavior and incidents identified by law enforcement officials and counterterrorism experts from across the country as being reasonably indicative of criminal activity associated with terrorism. In particular, the support from the following associations has been key to delivering the training and receiving reporting numbers:

- Association of State Criminal Investigative Agencies
- International Association of Chiefs of Police
- Major Cities Chiefs Association
- Major County Sheriffs' Association
- National Fusion Center Association
- National Sheriffs' Association

Because of the efforts of those involved with these associations, the NSI PMO was able to increase the number of line officers trained to approximately

250,000 in 2011. NSI staff will continue to partner with and conduct outreach to these agencies in the coming year to increase that number, with the goal of reaching every line officer across the country.

> This was taken from testimony provided by the Executive Director of the National Fusion Center Association to the House Appropriations Subcommittee on Homeland Security.
>
> A local police officer in Alabama made a traffic stop. Based on plain-sight observations, the officer asked to see the contents of a duffle bag in the back seat. Inside the duffle bag were four police uniforms and four police badges. When interviewed, each of the occupants stated they were headed to a location in Colorado, but each gave a different story. Beyond the traffic violation, there was no illegal activity, and the occupants were allowed to go on their way. What happened next shows how far we have come in taking proactive measures to protect the United States. The officer completed a report and clicked the "SAR" button available in the Alabama reporting system. That SAR went immediately to the Alabama Fusion Center, which analyzed the information and then contacted the fusion center in Colorado—the Colorado Information Analysis Center. Both of these fusion centers have an FBI presence.
>
> As of April 2012, the matter of this incident is still being considered. Whether this situation has to do with terrorism or some other criminal activity, the key point is that within *HOURS*, federal, state, and local officials who can act to *PREVENT* criminal activity were aware of the situation. This goes far beyond information sharing—this is deep collaboration that makes our country safer, and the fusion centers enable it.

Georgia and Arizona POST Credit for NSI Line Officer Training

To help deliver the SAR Line Officer Training to all officers in a timely manner, state and local law enforcement agencies in Arizona and Georgia have worked to cultivate relationships with the Peace Officer Standards and Training (POST) associations to advance the SAR training message through the state POST requirements process. The Georgia Bureau of Investigation has made it possible for all line officers to receive POST credit for viewing the NSI Line Officer Training video as part of their annual in- service POST requirement and has also included the Criminal Intelligence Coordinating Council privacy training, *The Importance of Privacy, Civil Rights, and Civil Liberties Protections in American Law Enforcement and Public Safety* video.

This action will lead to an increase in the number of officers in the state of Georgia who take the SAR Line Officer Training, as well as help to increase privacy protections. The same is expected in Arizona, where law enforcement has followed the lead set by Georgia and has made a submission to the Arizona POST Board for credit and curriculum approval. Arizona law enforcement officials are awaiting approval and hope to have the SAR Line Officer Training added soon to the cadre of training courses that are eligible to receive POST credits. The NSI will continue to facilitate the growth of the SAR training programs through both national POST contacts and states that adopt the program for state POST credits.

U.S. Department of Homeland Security—SAR Analytics

DHS SAR Analysis Project

The DHS SAR Analysis Project, which is managed by the Office of Intelligence and Analysis (I&A) Terrorist Targets and Tactics Branch, started as an effort to establish baseline metrics and evaluate the analytic value of the SAR in the NSI Federated Search. Since July 2011, the SAR team at DHS has conducted analysis and has begun developing a baseline of the reporting in the NSI for use in future analysis to assess any patterns, trends, tactics, techniques, and procedures. The analysts have been conducting a review and assessment of a representative sample of SAR information that was submitted through the NSI, including submissions made directly to the eGuardian system. This effort also advances DHS I&A all-source analysis, providing support for requests for information across DHS divisions, as well as external state and local support requests (SLSRs), NSI-derived production of Roll Call Releases, and support to other products, including joint-seal products with fusion centers.

DHS Roll Call Release Products Integrating SAR Data

SAR information is currently being leveraged by both state and local law enforcement, as well as national security organizations, in an all-source analysis effort intended to help secure the homeland. A significant benefit of the NSI lies in making SAR readily available to analysts who can inform the interagency homeland security community about evolving trends and criminal schemes, collate reported data with current threat streams, and show nationwide aggregated metrics of SAR across regions and infrastructure sectors.

As part of this effort, DHS I&A is integrating SAR into the interagency "Roll Call Release" (RCR) product line to inform its customers of key issues relevant to homeland security. This one-page, for-official-use- only product, which is produced jointly with the FBI and the Interagency Threat Assessment and Coordination Group (ITACG), can be quickly read and presents key points to inform, highlight, and raise awareness of ongoing threats; general concepts of illicit activity; and documentation of actual incidents. RCRs are proving to be a viable intelligence product through which SAR information can be reported to various partners.

Several RCRs were released in the beginning of 2012 as part of a series that addresses the NSI-defined indicators and behaviors of potential terrorist preoperational attack planning. In addition to the NSI definition and specific activities associated with the indicator and behavior, the RCRs also provide actual examples of SARs that were submitted to the NSI that illustrate these indicators and behaviors.

TECHNOLOGY IMPROVEMENTS

The NSI PMO made several improvements to the NSI Federated Search over the past year and has also provided resources for users to turn to for assistance, if needed.

Single Line Search

Similar to a Google search, the NSI Federated Search Tool provides a user with the ability to enter search parameters in an unstructured entry called the Single Line Search. In addition, the Single Line Search provides broader search parameters than previously available on the Advanced NSI Search Tool, which will help analysts find the information they need in a more efficient, expedient manner. A review of how to input search terms into the Single Line Search has been included in the NSI Analyst Technical Assistance that is provided by the Executive Support Specialists, and instructions are also provided in the updated NSI Federated Search User Manual.

Subscription Service

NSI Federated Search users can now create and save queries, also known as a subscription service, by utilizing the NSI user console. These queries can be saved to run on a recurring basis, identify other users searching the same criteria, and identify when a new SAR is submitted that contains the information saved in the data query. The user console can be accessed from any NSI search or results screen. Detailed instructions and examples of the subscription service feature are provided in the updated NSI Federated Search User Manual.

NSI Analytics

One reason the NSI Federated Search was developed was to share SARs and allow fusion centers, the FBI, and other agencies to review shared SARs so that analysts could potentially link behaviors and activities together with current threat information in an effort to prevent terrorism. As the NSI program expanded and input was received from the users of the NSI Federated Search Tool, a demand arose for the ability to view SAR at a higher level than searching a specific set of terms or criteria. To address this desire from the field and make the data being provided by all the NSI partners more user-friendly, an NSI Analytical Tool has been developed and will be released in 2012. This tool allows NSI users to:

- Review all SAR information submitted by each fusion center as an NSI Summary. These can be viewed by activity, threat, and/or infrastructure.
- Review SARs for a specific fusion center by activity, threat, and infrastructure.
- Search SARs for one or multiple activity types, threat codes, and/or infrastructure codes. This search will inform the user about the number of SARs that can be viewed based on the different combinations of items selected, allowing the user to select a combination of items and view all the SAR information that resulted from that combination.
- Compare across multiple NSI users for a specific activity, threat, or infrastructure.

- View a summary of what types of SARs a fusion center is handling based on activity, threat, or infrastructure.

Shared Space—eGuardian Information Sharing—eGuardian Web Service

In an attempt to bring all the facets of the NSI program together, the NSI PMO, working in conjunction with the eGuardian staff, has implemented a capability so that fusion centers electronically push NSI SAR from the fusion centers' local NSI common box to the FBI's eGuardian system.

This migration was done by utilizing the eGuardian Web service, which enables not only the push of an NSI SAR to eGuardian but also the immediate receipt of an eGuardian identification number for future reference.

Based on the feedback from fusion center directors, the NSI implemented a technical ability for a fusion center to push SAR information not only to the NSI Federated Search but simultaneously to eGuardian within a very short time of the fusion center's decision to share that NSI SAR.

> In May 2010, the FBI's Virtual Threat Analysis Center (VTAC) received a tip from the Barnesville, Georgia, Police Department that an unknown caller was making bomb threats.
>
> This information was entered into eGuardian, and then, through an automated process, the incident was placed into Guardian.
>
> A full investigation was initiated by FBI Atlanta, Macon Resident Agency, special agents, and within 72 hours, Satish Kumar Patel was arrested. Mr. Patel was charged with three counts of false public alarm, domestic terrorism, four counts of terroristic threats, and two counts of unlawful conduct during an emergency call.
>
> He pled guilty to three counts of making threats to damage buildings by means of fire or explosives.

NSI Help Desk

The NSI Help Desk and Knowledge Base is a secure site that allows users to find information regarding frequently asked questions (FAQs) pertaining to the NSI program.

Through this site, users can search a database of SAR-related FAQs, submit additional FAQs to the database, find helpful links and points of contact, view training documents and podcasts, and request additional assistance from the Help Desk.

Frequently Asked Questions

The FAQs—commonly asked SAR-related questions and answers—may be technical, procedural, or policy-oriented in nature. Examples of FAQ topics include but are not limited to Federated Search; baseline capabilities; privacy, civil rights, and civil liberties compliance; standard operating procedures and guidelines for fusion centers; Information Exchange Package Documentation (IEPD); NIEM; fusion center technical assistance; and predictive analytics. FAQs are often submitted to the NSI Help Desk but may also be submitted to the NSI PMO and support team through e-mails, calls, letters, and requests for technical assistance.

Conclusion

The NSI has continued to make major improvements in sharing terrorism-related information across the country, mostly due to the many federal, state, local, tribal, and territorial partners, national and international law enforcement associations, and reaching out beyond the law enforcement community to include new stakeholders to the overall mission.

This was evidenced by the release of the Unified Message, which provides a clear message to the field that there is a single, coordinated effort to encourage the reporting of suspicious activity and to share this information with the departments and agencies that need it to help keep our country safe from terrorism.

The endorsement of this document by a wide cross-section of key departments, national and international associations, and major agencies is an enormous accomplishment.

The addition of the NSI PMO Executive Support Specialists has been crucial in the advanced deployment of the NSI. Their expertise and hands-on support to NSI sites across the country have allowed fusion centers to expedite implementation of NSI processes and has allowed the NSI PMO to exceed expectations on deployment.

The NSI PMO expanded partnerships, developing many relationships with public safety organizations and associations which have helped promote and endorse the NSI, particularly with the SAR Hometown Security Partners Training.

Based upon this past year's progress, the NSI plans to expand its partnerships to other public safety agencies and organizations while continuing to maintain the existing relationships with those who have supported the mission since the beginning.

The NSI PMO is enthusiastic to build upon the hard work and foundations established in the past year and looks forward to the successes of the future.

APPENDIX 1. RESOURCES

NSI and SAR-related resources can be accessed at http://nsi.ncirc.gov/resources.aspx.

NSI Overview

Provides an overview of the Nationwide Suspicious Activity Reporting (SAR) Initiative (NSI).

Unified Message

This Unified Message document, issued in April 2012, was created to help clarify a unified approach to the process of reporting and sharing information related to suspicious activity.

NSI Training Overview

Provides a description of the multifaceted approach to the NSI training strategy, which includes training programs for frontline officers, analysts, and chief executives, as well as SAR awareness training for partners with similar missions to those of law enforcement constituencies.

NSI Hometown Security Partners

This document is an overview of the SAR Hometown Security Partners Training strategy, which provides SAR awareness training for partners with similar missions to those of law enforcement constituencies, or "hometown security partners."

NSI Technology Fact Sheet

Provides an overview of the technology used within the NSI and includes technical diagrams for the ISE-SAR Shared Space.

Privacy, Civil Rights, and Civil Liberties Protections: A Key Component of the Nationwide Suspicious Activity Reporting (SAR) Initiative (NSI)

Provides an overview of the privacy, civil rights, and civil liberties protections which serve as a foundational element of the NSI and which are required to participate.

ISE-SAR Functional Standard

Builds upon, consolidates, and standardizes nationwide aspects of those ISE-relevant activities already occurring at the federal, state, and local levels with respect to the processing, sharing, and use of suspicious activity information.

Suspicious Activity Reporting Process Implementation Checklist

Provides a simplified checklist for chief executives and senior leadership to implement a SAR process within their agencies.

State and Local Anti-Terrorism Training (SLA

Provides an overview of the SLATT database, which allows users to track terrorism trends, identify areas of high activity, and match terrorism pre-incident indicators against similar cases, both past and present.

Final Report: Information Sharing Environment (ISE)—Suspicious Activity Reporting (SAR) Evaluation Environment

Provides lessons learned, best practices, and implementation steps identified during the ISE-SAR Evaluation Environment that can be utilized while implementing the NSI.

Policy Resources

Nationwide SAR Initiative Annual Report 2010

This report provides an overview of the first 12 months of the Nationwide Suspicious Activity Reporting (SAR) Initiative (NSI) and features the program's foundation, success, and future growth.

Suspicious Activity Reporting Process Implementation Checklist

Provides a simplified checklist for chief executives and senior leadership to implement a SAR process within their agencies.

Nationwide Suspicious Activity Reporting Initiative Concept of Operations

Provides a common understanding of the NSI process so that implementation activities can be planned, executed, and measured.

Final Report: Information Sharing Environment (ISE)—Suspicious Activity Reporting (SAR) Evaluation Environment

Provides lessons learned, best practices, and implementation steps identified during the ISE-SAR Evaluation Environment that can be utilized while implementing the NSI.

Findings and Recommendations of the SAR Support and Implementation Project

This report and its recommendations are important for establishing national guidelines that will improve the identification and reporting of suspicious activity and will allow for the timely sharing of SAR information with law enforcement agencies, fusion centers, and the Joint Terrorism Task Forces (JTTFs).

National Strategy

Sets forth a national plan to build upon progress and establish a more integrated information sharing capability.

Privacy Resources

NSI Privacy Fact Sheet

This fact sheet provides an overview of the various components of the NSI Privacy Protection Framework, which is an integral element to the protection of privacy throughout the SAR process and to the overall success of the NSI.

Updated Privacy Policy Review Process

This document details the new privacy policy review process. It has been recently modified to support fusion centers and expedite the finalization of their privacy policies.

Fact Sheet: Privacy, Civil Rights, and Civil Liberties Analysis and Recommendations Report for the Nationwide Suspicious Activity Reporting (SAR) Initiative (NSI)

This fact sheet provides a brief background on the NSI and a description of the privacy, civil rights, and civil liberties framework. It also lists highlights and observations and details recommendations for NSI implementation.

The Nationwide Suspicious Activity (SAR) Reporting Initiative (NSI) Privacy, Civil Rights, and Civil Liberties Analysis and Recommendations

This report provides an update to the Initial Privacy and Civil Liberties Analysis published in September 2008. It contains a review of the development and implementation of the now concluded Information Sharing Environment Suspicious Activity Reporting (SAR) Evaluation Environment (EE) and makes recommendations to be followed during the nationwide implementation of the NSI.

Privacy, Civil Rights, and Civil Liberties Protections: A Key Component of the Nationwide Suspicious Activity Reporting (SAR) Initiative (NSI)

Provides an overview of the privacy, civil rights, and civil liberties protections which serve as a foundational element of the NSI and which are required to participate.

Technology Resources

NSI Technology Fact Sheet

Provides an overview of the technology used within the NSI and includes technical diagrams for the ISE-SAR Shared Space.

ISE-SAR Functional Standard

Builds upon, consolidates, and standardizes nationwide aspects of those ISE-relevant activities already occurring at the federal, state, and local levels with respect to the processing, sharing, and use of suspicious activity information.

Enterprise Architecture Program

This document laid the foundation in defining practices and methodologies required to build implementable and executable information sharing enterprise architectures and to segment architectures leveraging core ISE principles.

National Information Exchange Model (NIEM)

NIEM is designed to develop, disseminate, and support enterprise-wide information exchange standards and processes that can enable jurisdictions to effectively share critical information in emergency situations, as well as support the day-to-day operations of agencies throughout the nation.

eGuardian Privacy Impact Assessment

Training Resources

LEAPS.TV Overview

This document gives a brief overview of the Law Enforcement And Public Safety (LEAPS.TV) channel online, as well as instructions on how to access and view the SAR Line Officer Training CD through the LEAPS.TV Web site.

MIPT InCOP Overview

This document briefly describes the Memorial Institute for the Prevention of Terrorism's (MIPT) Information Collection on Patrol (InCOPSM) workshop series. These workshops progressively enhance intelligence capability, both in traditional crime and terrorism prevention. InCOP 1, the first of the four courses, builds upon and reinforces the processes and policies for gathering, documenting, processing, analyzing, and sharing information about terrorism-related suspicious activities, which is the core of the Nationwide Suspicious Activity Reporting Initiative.

FBI

Other Resources

State and Local Anti-Terrorism Training (SLA

The SLATT Program provides law enforcement personnel with specialized training and resources to combat terrorism and extremist criminal activity. A user name and password are required to access the SLATT Web site. To request a user name and password, please complete the Web site registration form.

ISE in the News

The Information Sharing Environment frequently posts articles about ISE Mission Partners. As a part of the ISE fabric, the NSI is often highlighted in these articles.

APPENDIX 2. COMMUNITY OUTREACH RESOURCES

Guidance for Building Communities of Trust

The Building Communities of Trust (BCOT) guidance provides advice and recommendations on how to initiate and sustain trusting relationships that support meaningful sharing of information, responsiveness to community concerns and priorities, and the reporting of suspicious activities that appropriately distinguish between innocent cultural behaviors and behavior that may legitimately reflect criminal enterprise or terrorism precursor activities. The guidance was developed in partnership with select sites that participated in the Nationwide SAR Initiative (NSI) Evaluation Environment.

Building Communities of Trust: A Guidance for Community Leaders

This document is a complementary piece to the *Guidance for Building Communities of Trust*, and was developed to assist community leaders working with law enforcement agencies to facilitate dialogue and discuss ways to work together to prevent crime and terrorism.

Communities Against Terrorism

Through the Communities Against Terrorism program, law enforcement agencies develop partnerships with their local business community to educate them on how to recognize terrorism/extremism warning signs and how to share the information with the right organization in order to prevent terrorism. To assist law enforcement agencies with their outreach efforts, various brochures are available for download on the SLATT Web site. To request a username and password for the SLATT Web site, please complete the Web site registration form.

APPENDIX 3. UNIFIED MESSAGE

A Call to Action: A Unified Message Regarding the Need to Support Suspicious Activity Reporting and Training is included on the following two pages.

A Call to Action:

A Unified Message Regarding the Need to Support Suspicious Activity Reporting and Training

Efforts to address crime and threats in our communities are most effective when they involve strong collaboration between law enforcement and the communities and citizens they serve. As a law enforcement or homeland security professional, you understand that *Homeland Security Is Hometown Security*.[1] Local, state, tribal, territorial, campus, and federal representatives are united in efforts to make our country safer.

One of these efforts relates to Suspicious Activity Reporting. To address this issue, in 2011, the International Association of Chiefs of Police (IACP) hosted a meeting of representatives from numerous local, state, and federal agencies and law enforcement organizations to create a unified approach to reporting and sharing suspicious activity.

As a result, these leaders have partnered to support a strategy that will unify the efforts of all agencies and organizations involved in the Nationwide Suspicious Activity Reporting (SAR) Initiative (NSI). The overall effort focuses on (1) increasing public awareness of reporting suspicious activity to law enforcement, (2) generating Suspicious Activity Reports by law enforcement, (3) analysis conducted by fusion centers and Federal Bureau of Investigation (FBI) Field Intelligence Groups (FIGs), and (4) investigation by the FBI's Joint Terrorism Task Forces (JTTFs).

As a law enforcement or homeland security professional, you are responsible to ensure that the public you serve understands how to report suspicious activity and that your agency/organizational members support the collection, analysis, and submission of Suspicious Activity Reports to your fusion center or FBI/JTTFs.

Fusion centers, FIGs, and JTTFs will share Suspicious Activity Reports seamlessly. The NSI Program Management Office (NSI PMO) and the FBI made technical adjustments in 2011 to ensure interoperability between the eGuardian and Shared Space systems. Suspicious Activity Reports entered into either system will be expeditiously pushed into the other automatically for sharing with other partners within the NSI as appropriate.

Detailed below are key points and action items that all law enforcement and homeland security personnel should be aware of, support, and institutionalize within their area of responsibility:

Reporting Suspicious Activities

- Agencies at all levels of government should utilize the "If You See Something, Say Something™" program to raise public awareness of indicators of terrorism and to emphasize the importance of reporting suspicious activity to the proper law enforcement authorities, while protecting privacy, civil rights, and civil liberties. (See "Outreach Activities" below for more details.)
- The public should contact law enforcement via 9-1-1 when an immediate response is needed regarding suspicious activity for any type of crime, including terrorism.
- Personnel from your agency should prepare Suspicious Activity Reports and forward them to fusion centers or FBI/JTTFs for follow-up and mutual coordination/deconfliction.
- Other potentially terrorism-related tips or leads reported directly to FBI/JTTFs will be evaluated for investigation, coordination, and entry into the NSI as appropriate.

1 *From Hometown Security to Homeland Security, IACP's Principles for a Locally Designed and Nationally Coordinated Homeland Security Strategy*, International Association of Chiefs of Police, http://www.theiacp.org/LinkClick.aspx?fileticket=78X8uKjLa0U%3D&tabid=392.

United States Department of Justice

Nationwide Suspicious Activity Reporting (SAR) Initiative (NSI)

- The NSI establishes standardized processes and policies that provide the capability for local, state, tribal, territorial, campus, and federal law enforcement to share timely, relevant Suspicious Activity Reports while working to ensure that privacy, civil rights, and civil liberties are protected.
- There are multiple options for entry of Suspicious Activity Reports.

SAR Training

- It is important to ensure that your agency's personnel have received the frontline officer training on identifying and reporting those behaviors that are potentially indicative of terrorist or other criminal activity while emphasizing the protection of privacy, civil rights, and civil liberties. This training is coordinated by the NSI, the U.S. Department of Homeland Security (DHS), the FBI, the IACP, and others for nationwide implementation and is available online via these sites:
    - NSI Web site: http://nsi.ncirc.gov/sarlot/
    - LEAPS.TV: http://www.leaps.tv/programdetail.php?program_code=201008031500
    - MIPT: http://www.mipt.org/SARTraining.aspx

It is vitally important that law enforcement agencies conduct SAR training with all law enforcement personnel, including supervisors, and document completion. Officers, chiefs, sheriffs, training officials, and other executives should integrate SAR training into initial and recurring training curricula.

Fusion Centers, FIGs, and JTTFs

- Fusion centers serve as focal points within the state and local environment for the receipt, analysis, gathering, and sharing of threat-related information among local, state, tribal, territorial, and federal partners. They produce actionable intelligence for dissemination, which can aid other law enforcement organizations, including the JTTFs, in their investigative operations.
- JTTFs are multiagency task forces designed to combine the resources, talents, skills, and knowledge of local, state, tribal, territorial, and federal law enforcement, as well as the Intelligence Community, into a single team that investigates and/or responds to terrorist threats. JTTFs investigate Suspicious Activity Reports and other terrorism tips and leads.
- FIGs, the hub of the FBI's intelligence program in the field, are the primary mechanism through which field offices identify, evaluate, and prioritize threats within their territories. Using dissemination protocols, FIGs contribute to regional and local perspectives on threats and serve as an important link between fusion centers, the FBI/JTTFs, and the Intelligence Community.

Outreach Activities

- The "If You See Something, Say Something™" public awareness campaign is a simple and effective program to raise public awareness of indicators of terrorism and violent crime.
- DHS uses "If You See Something, Say Something™" with permission from the New York Metropolitan Transportation Authority. Agencies, companies, or groups interested in partnering with DHS on this campaign should contact the DHS Office of Public Affairs at (202) 282-8010.

In: Nationwide Suspicious Activity …
Editor: Laurits Hartmann
ISBN: 978-1-62618-766-5
© 2013 Nova Science Publishers, Inc.

Chapter 4

NATIONWIDE SUSPICIOUS ACTIVITY REPORTING INITIATIVE: STATUS REPORT*

INTRODUCTION

> "Law enforcement has excellent information gathering techniques and skills in place. However, in order for that information to be useful, it must be shared. Simply put, the heart of this initiative is to glean information from routine police work for the fusion centers so that they may provide the analysis and intelligence that is critical to our efforts against crime and terrorism."
>
> - Commissioner Gerald Bailey, Florida Department of Law Enforcement

This status report on the Nationwide Suspicious Activity Reporting (SAR) Initiative (NSI) provides a summary assessment of the ISE-SAR Evaluation Environment over the last two years, highlighting four key findings and identifying a number of valuable lessons- learned. The report also provides specific recommendations to help guide the broader NSI implementation as it begins in 2010.

Over the last two years, federal, state, and local organizations have developed, tested, and evaluated the policies, procedures, and technology concepts needed to implement a unified process for gathering, documenting, processing, analyzing, and sharing suspicious activity reports that are

* This is an edited, reformatted and augmented version of the NSI Status Report, dated February 2010.

determined to be reasonably indicative of criminal activity associated with terrorism. The Evaluation Environment provided a controlled environment where agencies could evaluate potential solutions to operational challenges and identify best practices to be incorporated as part of a broader nationwide implementation. Although the Evaluation Environment period drew to a close at the end of Fiscal Year 2009, the operational process established at the participating agencies remains in place and sites continue to share ISE-SARs on a regular basis as part of the NSI. Additional sites are already being incorporated into the process even as the plans for a full nationwide implementation are developed.

This report provides an overview of the results of the Evaluation Environment as of November 2009. In addition, two related reports will be issued in early 2010:

1. The Program Manager for the Information Sharing Environment (PM-ISE)—in consultation with the Civil Liberties and Privacy Office of the Director of National Intelligence (DNI), the Office of Privacy and Civil Liberties of the Department of Justice (DOJ), and the Legal Issues Working Group of the ISE Privacy Guidelines Committee (PGC)—is preparing an updated *NSI Privacy, Civil rights, and Civil Liberties Analysis* that provides a more detailed view of this critical aspect of NSI implementation, and
2. The PM-ISE and the DOJ Bureau of Justice Assistance (BJA), with input from state and local law enforcement, fusion center personnel, and community advocates, are developing guidance for local law enforcement and fusion centers on developing trust relationships with community representatives based on the lessons-learned from the *Building Communities of Trust* initiative. This initiative aims to build bridges and mutual understanding among community groups, local law enforcement agencies, and state and major urban area fusion centers as a way of better protecting our local communities. The outcome is for law enforcement officers, public safety personnel, community leaders, and citizens to be better able to distinguish between innocent cultural behaviors and behavior indicative of criminal activity; and for local communities to play a more supportive role in combating terrorism-related crime. This effort is discussed in more detail in the Lessons-Learned section of this report.

Appendix A provides a comprehensive list of documents relating to the NSI.

KEY FINDINGS

> After SAR training had been conducted at one of the evaluation environment agencies, the site passed on information to local police departments on how to recognize and report SARs to the fusion center for further vetting. One department—not directly involved in the ISE-SAR Evaluation Environment—received a tip submitted by a member of the public that previously might have been ignored. Because the police department had received training on how to identify and report potential terrorism-related suspicious activity the information was sent directly to the Fusion Center for further review. Fusion Center analysts vetted the information, determined that it did have a potential nexus to terrorism, and forwarded the information. That would not have otherwise gone, to the Joint Terrorism Task Force (JTTF). The information provided a key link in an ongoing JTTF investigation.

The major results from the ISE-SAR Evaluation Environment can be summarized in the following four key findings.

1. A Clear, Positive Impact on Local Counterterrorism Efforts

The ISE-SAR Evaluation Environment demonstrated the value of a standardized SAR process in supporting the counterterrorism efforts of state and local law enforcement agencies.

The NSI cycle includes specific steps that better enable local law enforcement agencies to leverage knowledge provided by the Federal Government on terrorist tactics, techniques, and plans. This knowledge is then used to improve training provided to frontline officers, investigators, and analysts so they are better able to recognize behaviors and incidents indicative of terrorism-related criminal activity. There are examples from Evaluation Environment sites where the proper submission of a SAR led to investigations, arrests, prosecutions, or informant recruiting.

2. It is Possible to Combat Terrorism While Protecting Privacy

The ISE-SAR Evaluation Environment showed that it is possible to combat terrorism effectively and protect privacy, civil rights, and civil liberties. Moreover, it reinforced the principle that local implementation of a uniform NSI Privacy, Civil Rights, and Civil Liberties Framework is critical to successful NSI implementation and provides a national benefit.

All participants in the ISE-SAR Evaluation Environment were required to implement a robust, all-inclusive approach for maximizing the protection of privacy, civil rights, and civil liberties before being allowed to share or access ISE-SAR information. The requirements underlying this NSI Privacy, Civil Rights, and Civil Liberties Framework evolved over the course of the Evaluation Environment.[1] They include:

a. The NSI process at each participating agency must be conducted under statutory authorities and departmental privacy and civil liberties policies and procedures that are consistent with the ISE Privacy Guidelines.[2] Each participating agency must submit privacy and civil liberties policies and procedures for review to ensure consistency with the ISE Privacy Guidelines prior to sharing personal information (i.e., privacy fields) to the ISE Shared Space.
b. Implementation must include training of front line officers, investigators, analysts, and supervisors regarding the behaviors and indicators of terrorism related criminal activity.
c. Each participating agency must put in place a formal, multi-layered vetting process in which each SAR is reviewed by a supervisor and an experienced investigator or analyst specifically trained in counter-terrorism issues before it is designated as an ISE-SAR.
d. Sites should engage in outreach and collaboration at a local level with privacy and civil liberty advocacy groups.

Although participating agencies found the implementation of this Framework to be a formidable undertaking, they agreed that the NSI process could be implemented practically while still maintaining required privacy, civil rights, and civil liberties protections. Adoption of the NSI Privacy Framework as a foundation of the nationwide implementation should engender public trust by ensuring that participating law enforcement agencies across the country adopt standard processes, policies, and procedures for protecting privacy, civil rights, and civil liberties that are at least as comprehensive as those required for federal agencies by the *ISE Privacy Guidelines*.[3]

3. Inter-Agency Sharing of ISE-SARs Continues to Show Potential

Indications from ISE-SAR Evaluation Environment participants and other sources suggest that the sharing of SAR information between neighboring localities and within regions improves their ability to identify trends indicative of terrorism-related criminal activity. It is also likely that, under a certain set of conditions, the ability of DHS and Federal Bureau of Investigation (FBI) analysts to search local repositories would be beneficial as well. Because of the unanticipated length of time it took to ensure the NSI Privacy Framework was in place, there was a relatively short timeframe during which sites were able to operationally share ISE-SAR information across agencies. Nevertheless, although it was not possible to quantitatively evaluate this aspect of the SAR process, qualitative evidence gathered in discussions with participants supports the conclusion that interagency sharing will ultimately prove useful.

Agencies participating in the ISE-SAR Evaluation Environment were not authorized to share SAR data with other sites until they had met the requirements of the NSI Privacy Framework. The unanticipated length of time required to develop and implement privacy policies and procedures as part of the Framework limited the period during which most sites were able to share ISE-SARs to a few months at most. This turned out to be too short a period to amass sufficient data to quantify the value of sharing regionally and nationally. However, based on the experience of several sites that demonstrated expanded intra-regional sharing during the Evaluation Environment, the consensus view is that the ability to conduct predicated searches at regional and national levels will ultimately enhance the national capability to identify patterns and trends indicative of terrorism activity or other criminal activity associated with terrorism.

4. The NSI Process is Applicable to an All-Crimes Environment

Though the focus of the ISE-SAR Evaluation Environment is sharing terrorism-related suspicious activity, the standardized approach can apply to all types of crime.

The ISE-SAR Evaluation Environment was focused on SARs indicative of terrorism- related crimes; but both the steps in the NSI cycle and the data elements in the ISE- SAR Functional Standard are directly applicable or can be easily adapted to other types of criminal behavior. Almost all of the participating Evaluation Environment sites already operate in an “all crimes” environment where terrorism is only one of a number of criminal behaviors to which gathering and sharing of SARs may be applicable. In fact, many participating agencies noted that the standardized NSI process enhanced their ability to gather, document, process, analyze, and share other types of criminal information as well. In particular, the process may be especially effective for gang and drug-related crimes. Some additional steps will be necessary to incorporate additional suspicious behavior types, to include:

a. Changes to the NSI CONOPS and the ISE-SAR Functional Standard; and
b. Review of the privacy, civil rights, and civil liberties policies and procedures developed for the Evaluation Environment to ensure they are applicable in an all- crimes environment.

These qualifications notwithstanding, applying the NSI process to other types of criminal activities should be considered part of the logical progression for the nationwide implementation.

BACKGROUND

The NSI builds on what law enforcement and other agencies have been doing for years—gathering information regarding behaviors and incidents associated with crime— and establishes a replicable process whereby SAR information can be shared to help detect and prevent terrorism-related criminal activity. It was developed pursuant to Presidential direction to establish a nation-wide capability to gather, document, process, analyze and share information about terrorism-related suspicious incidents to enable rapid identification and mitigation of potential terrorist threats.[4] The resulting process— usually referred to as the "NSI process" or the "NSI cycle"—is shown in Figure 1.

The NSI is collaboration among a number of stakeholders including the PM-ISE; DOJ and its components (in particular BJA and the FBI); the Departments of Homeland Security (DHS) and Defense (DoD); the Office of the Director of National Intelligence (ODNI); and state and local law enforcement officials from across the nation. In addition, a number of major law enforcement organizations—the Global Justice Criminal Intelligence Coordinating Council (CICC), the International Association of Chiefs of Police (IACP), the Major City Chiefs Association (MCCA), the National Sheriffs Association, and the Major County Sheriffs Association (MCSA)—formally endorsed the NSI and were key players in the effort to plan and carry out the ISE-SAR Evaluation Environment.

The major objective of the ISE-SAR Evaluation Environment was to establish, at each of the participating sites, policies and business processes that support the gathering, documenting, processing, analyzing, and sharing of SARs while also ensuring that privacy, civil rights, and civil liberties were adequately protected in accordance with federal, state, and local laws and regulations. As a condition of participation, agencies were required to implement the NSI Privacy Framework that included a requirement to train all involved personnel before posting or accessing ISE-SARs.

The PM-ISE developed a performance measurement implementation plan to gauge the effectiveness of the Evaluation Environment that included a set of discrete measures designed to assess the performance of the NSI process and associated technical solutions. The plan employed a number of techniques to collect information, including automated tools, interviews, and survey reporting by the sites, and will serve as the basis for a more permanent performance measurement plan to support nationwide implementation.

Although not all sites were able to report data for all of the measures, the plan did provide a common understanding of what was being evaluated, the reporting process, and individual responsibilities. Sites provided qualitative or quantitative results that indicated the potential utility of the NSI process to broader counterterrorism outcomes, including data on:

- Federal investigations initiated as a result of SARs;
- Local investigations initiated as a result of SARs;
- Local or federal investigations that led to arrests or convictions in cases involving SARs; and

- SARs used for critical infrastructure protection and that contributed to analytic products.

Twelve state or local and three federal agencies ultimately participated in the Evaluation Environment.[5] During the period covered by this report, not all participants were able to fully share SAR data because of the unanticipated length of time needed to satisfy NSI Privacy Framework requirements. As a result, there is now a better understanding of the required level of commitment and time required before full sharing can take place. As noted in the "Introduction" section of this report, the Evaluation Environment was formally concluded at the end of September 2009. But the operational process remains in place and sites continue to share ISE-SARs on a regular basis. Additional sites are already being incorporated into the process even as the plans for a full nationwide implementation are developed.

The Evaluation Environment identified a number of valuable lessons-learned that, in turn, helped generate best practices to be followed as part of the follow-on implementation of a nationwide process for SAR. The remainder of this report examines these lessons-learned and outlines specific recommendations to help guide the nationwide implementation effort beginning in 2010.

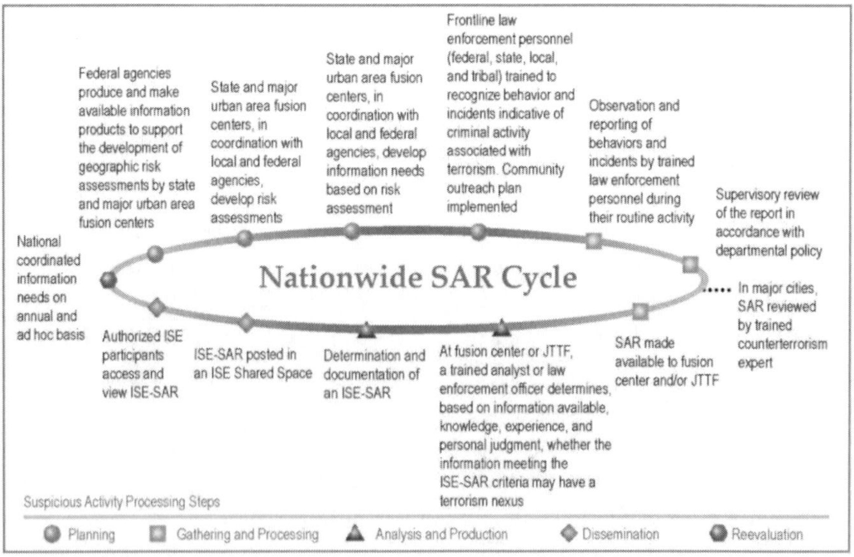

Figure 1. The Nationwide SAR Cycle.

LESSONS-LEARNED

At one participating agency, over 2,100 SARs have been reported by trained officers resulting in 167 referrals to the JTTF, 26 local terrorism cases opened, and 50 local arrests for other types of crimes.

The ISE-SAR Evaluation Environment provided a controlled environment to implement and assess standard processes for gathering, documenting, processing, analyzing, and sharing terrorism-related suspicious activity reports. It also produced enough results for the Federal Government to successfully evaluate the effectiveness of the NSI process on activities related to gathering, documenting, processing, and analyzing suspicious activities determined to be reasonably indicative of terrorism-related crimes. While the amount of information actually *shared* during the evaluation period was constrained by the limited number of participants and the timeframe involved, the Evaluation Environment demonstrated that the integrated NSI process works effectively and participating agencies experienced tangible benefits. This section highlights some important lessons-learned from the Evaluation Environment that contributed directly to the four key findings discussed above.

1. Executive Leadership is Essential

Evaluation Environment participants observed that executive sponsorship is critical to the successful adoption and implementation of a standard NSI process. For example, Chief Harold Hurtt of the Houston Police Department noted that "If you're not committed to it [the NSI] at the top of your organization, it's not going to happen. The officers may be introduced to it, but if there's not interest from the Chief or the person at the top of the organization, it won't be done properly." Specific approaches for ensuring leadership commitment varied among participating agencies, but they all agreed on the need to articulate clear mission expectations and provide adequate training for conducting the SAR mission, including the need to safeguard privacy, civil rights, and civil liberties. Several participating sites elected to issue special or general orders signed by senior leadership during the course of the ISE-SAR Evaluation Environment, an approach that proved valuable in demonstrating top-level management commitment to the effort.

2. NSI Implementation Must Leverage Existing Processes and Procedures

Law enforcement agencies have been gathering and documenting SAR information for years. As a result, to meet the goal of establishing and implementing a standard nationwide SAR process, the ISE-SAR Evaluation Environment was able to effectively leverage existing processes and procedures already in place at participating localities. In most cases, participating sites were able to simply modify existing procedures to implement the standard NSI process. The ISE-SAR Functional Standard, for example, does not prescribe the details of all processes, systems requirements, or other business rules governing the collection, processing, or sharing of SARs by law enforcement entities. Instead it provides a top-level process that builds on the well-established processes and business rules for suspicious activity reporting already in place at federal, state, local, and tribal agencies.

> One large urban Police Department added a check-box to its existing field interview forms to specifically denote a report as a SAR. This allowed the form to be properly routed for processing and, more importantly, did not require the frontline officer to fill out a new form. The training of the officers on behaviors potentially indicative of terrorism-related criminal activity was the only new element in their process.

By leveraging existing procedures and systems—building on the familiar—participating agencies were able to simplify the introduction of a new capability into their organizations, minimizing the impact on their processes and, most importantly, their people. Several sites have begun to institutionalize the use of SAR in their existing daily processes. One participating state fusion center has already incorporated the requirement to search both internal and external repositories of SAR information into its standard analytic process.

3. Personal Relationships Are Key When Introducing New Processes

Despite the intent to minimize the burden on Evaluation Environment sites, even the best planned implementations of new processes requires sufficient time for personnel to become familiar enough with them to integrate them into their day-to-day activities. In the interim, personal relationships continue to be important for maintaining continuity of operations. In fact, a significant conclusion drawn from the ISE-SAR Evaluation Environment was that improved processes and technology enhanced effectiveness, but did not substitute for personal relationships in collaborating and sharing information.

The NSI cycle involves a series of routine steps that are fairly mechanical and which can be completed strictly internal to the participating agency. There are some steps, however, that depend on close collaboration among federal, state, local, and tribal agencies. During the Evaluation Environment, information sharing worked best when local site and federal personnel were either collocated or at least near one another.

Assignment of federal personnel to participating sites or rotation of state, local, and tribal personnel to operational units at the federal headquarters level enhanced collaboration and information sharing. Sites that maintained close relations with local federal analysts enjoyed greater access to information—both pushed and pulled— because local analysts were better able to convey to the federal partner a clearer understanding of the site's priorities and information needs. Federal analysts, working with fusion center personnel were better able to collaborate on work products, develop threat and risk assessments, and share information. Collocation of personnel also helped improve the quality and effectiveness of federal products developed to meet state, local, and tribal requirements.

4. An Effective Training Program Is a Critical Element of Success

A well-developed and executed training program proved critical to the successful implementation of the SAR process. The NSI training program expands officers, investigators, and analysts' knowledge of behaviors and incidents indicative of terrorism-related criminal activity. This specialized training is important to the SAR process because, as noted in an important court case on this subject, conduct that may be innocuous when viewed in isolation can sometimes be determined to be suspicious when considered as part of the totality of the circumstances. [6] This guidance ensures that frontline law enforcement personnel, their supervisors, and the analysts who have responsibility for vetting SARs, have the proper context to make inferences about the cumulative information available to them, which enables them to carry out their responsibilities in accordance with laws, regulations, policies, and procedures that help safeguard privacy, civil rights, and civil liberties.[7]

> At the beginning of the ISE-SAR Evaluation Environment, several participants reported holding between several hundred and several thousand legacy SARs considered to be potentially terrorism-related. Sites reviewed their holdings in accordance with terrorism behaviors as described in the ISE SAR Functional Standard and described in the Analyst Vetting course and, as a result, reprocessed the information, and significantly reduced the volume of data considered to have a potential nexus to terrorism. One site was able to filter out almost 95 percent of its reports by determining that they had no terrorism nexus. Analyst training helps preclude having "too many dots" to sort through by ensuring only those with relevant analytical value are shared. Training also enabled analysts to better understand the utility of accessing numerous public, private, federal, state, and local data repositories to gain valuable information and to enhance their performance.

Accordingly, the NSI Project Team and its stakeholders—including BJA, FBI, DHS, IACP, MCCA, MCSA, and the National Sheriffs' Association—developed a specialized pilot training program specifically designed to address privacy, civil rights, and civil liberties safeguards. Members of the privacy, civil rights, and civil liberties advocacy community reviewed and provided valuable input to the three-part curriculum which included separate courses that provided specialized training targeted at three groups of people: executive-level personnel, frontline officers, and analysts.

The integrated training program was critical to establishing a standard NSI process. Significant results of the training included:

- A reduction in the number of SARs identified as potentially terrorism-related through better filtering;
- Improvement in the quality of SARs; and,
- An enhanced focus by all participants on ameliorating privacy, civil rights, and civil liberties.

As a result of the training program, frontline officers were better able to place observed or reported behaviors into context, maximizing their effectiveness in identifying potential criminal activity while minimizing the likelihood of documenting circumstances involving individuals engaged in innocent or constitutionally protected activities. Although there is insufficient data to draw definite conclusions, this suggests that training is improving the quality of reports from frontline officers and, consequently, making the analysts' jobs easier by providing them with higher quality inputs better conforming to the criteria in Part B of the ISE-SAR Functional Standard. More information is needed over the longer term to validate this observation.

5. Threat Information and Tactical Risk Assessments Should Drive State and Local Information Needs

A Congressional Research Service study on the NSI identifies a number of instances where police, acting in the normal course of their duties, arrested individuals who were acting suspiciously, and subsequently uncovered or disrupted terrorist plots.[8] An objective of the NSI process is that the discovery and disruption of these plots should not be merely a serendipitous result of unfocused information gathering but instead stem from an end-to-end process driven by clear information needs. Federal agencies must provide relevant threat information to state and local agencies that can contribute to local or regional threat and risk assessments and better inform local operational activity. To meet this objective, required steps include:

a. Identification and submittal of state and local information needs to appropriate agencies at the federal level;
b. Development of federal products in response to state and local information needs;
c. Completion of tactical risk assessments against potential threats; and
d. Guidance to frontline officers on tactics, techniques and behaviors indicative of terrorism activities.[9]

During the course of the Evaluation Environment, DHS and FBI worked closely with participating agencies to define a process that would capture and respond to state, local, and tribal information needs. The NSI Concept of Operations, published after the Evaluation Environment was already underway, established an approach for sharing Terrorism Information Needs among federal agencies and state, local, and tribal organizations.[10] This process is still in its early stages, but once fully implemented, will assist in enabling more thorough and focused risk assessments by state, local, and tribal law enforcement in partnership with the Federal Government.

> Based on an earlier case that the FBI solved in 2009, a major urban area fusion center refined the list of terrorism behaviors to watch for, updated training material, and briefed airport security personnel in the fusion center's area of responsibility. The result— attributable at least in part to better informed airport security personnel—has been more consistent and higher quality reports of relevant suspicious activity.

Tactical Risk Assessments are based in part on federal threat information about terrorist intentions, plans, and techniques. They add a local or regional dimension to that threat by examining the vulnerabilities of potential targets and assessing potential consequences should an attack be successful. Such assessments should result in improved information needs as well as better guidance to and more efficient use of public safety personnel to accomplish a more efficient allocation of limited resources. In addition, these assessments can contribute to frontline officer training by providing officers with the proper context within which to gather SAR information even where behavior may be seemingly innocent. For example, the act of photographing a bridge could take on more or less meaning and be met with a more informed and appropriate response when viewed in the context of current threat and risk assessments— the "totality of the circumstances" described in the earlier discussion on training.

Though not yet fully institutionalized, this front-end planning component of the NSI cycle has already demonstrated its value to the collection and reporting of information. During the course of the Evaluation Environment, state, local, and tribal agencies received Risk Assessment training using a case study based on the November 2008 terrorist attack in Mumbai where nearly 500 people were killed or injured. As a result of that training, a number of state, local, and tribal organizations are examining the risks to their critical infrastructure based on the terrorist tactics, techniques, and behaviors used in the attack.

6. Functional Standards Enable Effective Sharing of ISE-SARs

The steps in the NSI cycle can be implemented in a number of ways, but the overarching process itself is what drives how technology is used as an enabling capability. The Evaluation Environment helped drive home the essential point that underlying functional and technical standards serve as important enablers for effective sharing.

Regardless of the particular implementation, the basis for sharing in the NSI is the ISE- SAR Functional Standard. This standard describes a uniform process and associated data model to support the identification, documentation, and sharing of ISE-SAR information to the maximum extent possible consistent with the protection of privacy, civil rights, and civil liberties.[11] The standard provides the unifying glue that allows participating agencies with different technical implementations and systems to share information effectively and efficiently. It provides an important capability for representing details about terrorism-related suspicious activity in a standard format to help facilitate the identification of useful investigatory or trending information.

The NSI CONOPS describes a multilevel review process for identifying those SARs with a potential nexus to terrorism out of the thousands of suspicious activities documented by source agencies each day.[12] Following the gathering step and a preliminary review by a local agency, a trained analyst or law enforcement officer at a fusion center or federal agency first determines whether the suspicious activity meets any of the criteria set forth in Part B of the ISE-SAR Functional Standard. These criteria describe behaviors and incidents identified by law enforcement officials and counterterrorism experts from across the country as being reasonably indicative of criminal activity associated with terrorism. Following this, the analyst or officer then determines—based on a combination of knowledge, experience, other available information, and ultimately, personal judgment—whether the information is reasonably indicative of pre-operational planning related to terrorism. If this determination is made, the report will be documented in the data format and schema prescribed by the standard's Information Exchange Package Document (IEPD) and made available to all appropriate ISE participants through ISE Shared Spaces consistent with the NSI Privacy Framework.

The major implementation approach used during the Evaluation Environment relied on a distributed environment consisting of multiple ISE Shared Space servers at participant locations. Information loaded into the ISE Shared Space servers can be searched, accessed, and displayed by all authorized ISE investigative and analytic personnel to support their counterterrorism missions.[13] Information remains under the local control of the participating agency. Another technical solution is the FBI eGuardian system, which is available for use by state, local, and tribal agencies. Information entered into eGuardian is to be replicated in a separate eGuardian shared space server and made available to authorized NSI participants. Although eGuardian is based on different technology and provides other capabilities, its ISE Shared Space server functions—for information sharing purposes—like all the others. The Department of Defense has elected to enter its Force Protection SARs into eGuardian. Some state, local, and tribal agencies who have expressed interest in participating in the NSI are also already using or contemplating using eGuardian.

7. Sharing Must Be Accomplished in a Way that Protects Privacy, Civil Rights, and Civil Liberties

Fundamental to the success of the NSI is the commitment to protect privacy, civil rights, and civil liberties guaranteed by the Constitution and laws of the United States. Prior to the start of the ISE-SAR Evaluation Environment, the PM-ISE and its federal partners analyzed potential privacy and civil liberties risks associated with ISE-SAR information sharing activities and consulted with privacy and civil liberties advocacy groups to identify effective mitigation tools. This process culminated in the issuance of an initial analysis which identified two key objectives:

a. Revision and adoption of the ISE-SAR Functional Standard; and
b. Development of a robust privacy protection framework. [14]

The Functional Standard, as revised in May 2009, identifies the types of activity that may be deemed suspicious and the circumstances under which such information may be shared.[15] By focusing on observed behavior, this standard mitigates the risk of profiling based on race, ethnicity, national origin, or religion. It also improves mission effectiveness by enabling agencies to scope and address potential threats in a more efficient and standardized manner.

The second key objective led directly to the development of what ultimately became the NSI Privacy, Civil Rights, and Civil Liberties Framework described more fully under Key Finding 2. Before a site may share or receive personal information contained in privacy fields, the site must ensure that its written policies and procedures satisfy applicable ISE Privacy Guideline requirements, including: (a) purpose specification; (b) notice mechanisms; (c) data quality; (d) data security; (e) accountability/enforcement and audit; and (f) redress.[16]

The PM-ISE and its federal partners assisted the sites by developing privacy policy templates, offering technical assistance, and by reviewing each site's privacy policy. In addition, sites must ensure that all personnel are adequately trained before the process begins (see Lesson-Learned 4 for a fuller discussion).

Revision of the Functional Standard and adoption of what became the NSI Privacy Framework effectively mitigated implementation risks during the ISE-SAR Evaluation Environment as the following results show:

a. No complaints for redress were filed;
b. No sites reported a breach of personal information contained in privacy fields;
c. After spending approximately six months developing and implementing their privacy policies, nine sites had privacy policies approved and in place
d. Privacy awareness was heightened as a result of extensive training of site personnel and by requiring personnel to review and certify acceptance of the site's privacy policy; and
e. The outreach efforts to the public and to privacy and civil liberty advocacy groups at the beginning of the ISE-SAR Evaluation Environment facilitated the identification and mitigation of potential implementation risks.

Such results show that the NSI Privacy Framework adds value and can be successfully implemented. In particular, the extensive training provided to key personnel heightened awareness of basic privacy safeguards. This heightened awareness, when implemented nationally, will form a solid foundation for achieving a consistent, appropriate response by law enforcement to suspicious activity within their jurisdiction.

The broader NSI implementation should address the following features as part of implementing the NSI Privacy Framework:

a. Sites must fully implement the Framework prior to participation in the NSI;
b. Participating agencies should continually assess and update their privacy policies and procedures and ensure they are fully integrated into business processes;

c. Sites should establish personal accountability for protecting privacy, civil rights, and civil liberties for all site personnel and participating agencies;
d. The NSI Program Management Office should continue to provide technical assistance to sites to support privacy policy adoption and implementation; and
e. Sites should have a trained privacy officer available to provide ongoing advice and assistance regarding privacy, civil rights, and civil liberties.

All NSI stakeholders are committed to a transparent NSI process to foster public trust. In early 2010, the ISE Privacy Guidelines Committee (Chaired jointly by senior privacy officials from the ODNI, DOJ, and DHS) will publicly release a final in-depth privacy analysis of the NSI Evaluation Environment that will describe lessons-learned in more detail and provide specific recommendations for moving forward with the nationwide implementation.

8. Outreach and Collaboration with Community Leaders is Essential

NSI success depends heavily on the ability to earn and maintain the public's trust. Although outreach and collaboration with community representatives at the local level was not an explicit requirement of the ISE-SAR Evaluation Environment at the outset, the *Building Communities of Trust* initiative was developed and piloted in four of the Evaluation Environment sites to help achieve greater collaboration and transparency. The initiative aims to develop relationships of trust between police, fusion centers, and the communities they serve, particularly immigrant and minority communities, so that the challenges of crime control and terrorism prevention can be confronted with the support of local communities.

The Building Communities of Trust initiative brought together police, fusion center, and community representatives in a roundtable setting to help build trust-based relationships and increase understanding of different concerns and perspectives. The groups discussed specific local concerns and reviewed how NSI implementation and training will help law enforcement determine the difference between innocent cultural behaviors and behavior indicative of criminal activity. Findings from the project will be available in early 2010 and are being incorporated into NSI nationwide implementation.

RECOMMENDATIONS

The following recommendations are designed to assist with NSI implementation; many are interrelated and will need to be addressed as part of NSI PMO planning.

1. Establish a Program Management Office to Manage and Oversee NSI Implementation

Based on recent White House direction, NSI implementation will enter a new, more formal phase starting in 2010.[17] In response, DOJ is establishing an interagency NSI Program Management Office (PMO) to manage implementation. PMO participation will include DHS, FBI, and other federal, state, local and tribal partners. The PMO, in conjunction with all NSI stakeholders, should ensure that the lessons-learned from the Evaluation Environment and recommendations in this report are incorporated into future implementation activities.

2. Apply a Robust Framework to Protect Privacy, Civil Rights, and Civil Liberties

Protection of privacy, civil rights and civil liberties is essential to the success of the NSI process. Accordingly, consistent with Key Finding 2, all agencies participating in the NSI must implement a Privacy Framework that includes the following elements: (a) demonstration that operations are conducted in accordance with laws, policies, and procedures consistent with the ISE Privacy Guidelines; (b) training of frontline officers, investigators, analysts, and supervisors on the behaviors and indicators of terrorism- related criminal activity; (c) a formalized, multi-layered vetting process for SAR and ISE- SAR information; and (d) a program of outreach and collaboration to the community, including privacy, civil rights, and civil liberties advocacy groups at the local level.

3. Tailor Federal Information Products for Use by State, Local, and Tribal Agencies

Although state, local, and tribal sites participating in the ISE-SAR Evaluation Environment found value in some of the threat assessments received from federal agencies, in many cases the information was too general to drive the Risk Assessment and Information Needs steps of the NSI cycle. The Interagency Threat Assessment and Coordination Group (ITACG), situated within the National Counterterrorism Center (NCTC), should continue to work closely with DHS and the FBI to ensure that federal information products are sufficiently specific to meet the needs of state, local, and tribal agencies. DHS and FBI, with ITACG participation, should also continue to work with state, local and tribal partners to ensure that the list of priority terrorism-related information needs is periodically refreshed.

4. Institutionalize the NSI Risk Assessment Process

An important step in the NSI cycle requires state and major urban area fusion centers, working with local representatives of federal agencies, to develop tactical risk assessments of potential terrorist targets within their jurisdictions. While there were some attempts to address this requirement as part of the Evaluation Environment, they were limited. The NSI PMO—working with DHS as it stands up a National Fusion Center Program Management Office—should coordinate with all relevant stakeholders to develop and test a standard methodology for completing tactical risk assessments and use the results to help develop information needs.

5. Extend the NSI Process to an All Crimes Mission Environment

The focus of the NSI to date has been specifically on SARs indicative of terrorism- related crimes (i.e., ISE SARs). However, almost all participating agencies operate in an "all crimes" environment where terrorism is only one of a number of criminal behaviors to which gathering and sharing of SARs is applicable. Consistent with Key Finding 4, the NSI PMO—working with DHS, FBI, and NSI participants—should lead an effort to incorporate an all-crimes approach into the NSI.

6. Formalize NSI Feedback Mechanisms

Feedback is an important part of the NSI cycle. During the ISE-SAR Evaluation Environment, feedback was provided largely on an ad hoc basis. The NSI PMO— working with DHS, DoD, FBI, and NSI participants—should ensure that standardized feedback mechanisms are adopted that, at a minimum, notify: (a) "source organizations" when information they provide is designated as an ISE-SAR by a "submitting organization" and made available for sharing; and (b) participants when further evidence determines that an ISE-SAR was designated incorrectly so that the original information does not continue to be used as the basis for analysis or action.

7. Incorporate ISE-SARs into the Broader Analytic Process

During the Evaluation Environment, the focus was on posting, viewing, and sharing SAR information. But as the national implementation gets underway, it is important to think more broadly about how SARs can and should be used as one important information source in a larger analytic process. DHS and the National Fusion Center PMO—working with the NSI PMO, DOJ, FBI, NCTC and the ITACG, PM-ISE, and other NSI participants—should develop analytic tradecraft and a methodology that will lead to the effective use of ISE-SAR information as a contributor to the larger counterterrorism analytic process. In addition, the NSI PMO—working with DHS, FBI, and the PM-ISE— should develop a methodology that supports the organization and display of SAR information using analytic tools but still protects privacy, civil rights, and civil liberties and maintains control of the information by the submitting organization.

8. Establish Training for Mid-level Managers

Presentation of executive, frontline officer, and analyst training was fundamental to establishing the SAR process at participating sites and for ensuring the protection of privacy, civil rights, and civil liberties. However, as the evaluation progressed, it became increasingly apparent that mid-level managers, responsible for the daily direction and management of frontline officers, required equivalent training. The NSI PMO should ensure mid-level manager training is incorporated in future training plans and programs.

9. Establish a Performance Measurement Plan for NSI Implementation

A significant challenge faced by the PMO will be to establish effective performance criteria to measure the ultimate success of the NSI Program. Identifying appropriate metrics will be critical to determining outcomes. Performance plans should be reviewed to ensure they provide a results-oriented approach to monitor progress and performance, optimize resources, and promote accountability. While some output criteria may include data on the number of SARs produced and shared, the NSI PMO and all participating agencies should work to establish more mature indicators that support answers to target outcomes such as whether SARs produced and shared under the program are "meaningful," and whether sharing achieves the objective of ensuring the "dots are connected."

Appendix A. References

Available on PM-ISE Website (www.ise.gov)

Final Report on Presidential Guideline 2 – Develop a Common Framework for the Sharing of Information Between and Among Executive Departments and Agencies and State, Local, and Tribal Governments, Law Enforcement Agencies, and the Private Sector (approved by the President in November 2006), established a number of requirements that formed the basis for the initial ISE-SAR business process.

Final Report: Information Sharing Environment (ISE)-Suspicious Activity Reporting (SAR) Evaluation Environment, prepared by the Bureau of justice Assistance, (January 2010).

Findings and Recommendations of the Suspicious Activity Report (SAR) Support and Implementation Project (October 2008). A publication sponsored by BJA; MCCA; DOJ's Global Justice Information Sharing Initiative (Global), the CICC; DHS; and the FBI.

ISE-SAR Evaluation Environment Segment Architecture (December 2008).

ISE-SAR Functional Standard, Version 1.5, ISE-FS-200 (May 21, 2009).

ISE-SAR Functional Standard and Evaluation Environment Privacy and Civil Liberties Analysis (September 5, 2008).

National Strategy for Information Sharing: Successes and Challenges in Improving Terrorism-Related Information Sharing (October 2007).

Nationwide Suspicious Activity Reporting Initiative Concept of Operations (December 2008).

Others

Baseline Capabilities for State and Major Urban Area Fusions Centers: A Supplement to the Fusion Center Guidelines (September 2008) available at http://www.it.ojp.gov/default.aspx?area=globalJustice&page=1236

Fusion Center Guidelines: Law Enforcement Intelligence, Public Safety, and thePrivate Sector (October 2009), available at http://www.it.ojp.gov/default.aspx? area=globalJustice&page=1236

National Criminal Intelligence Sharing Plan, published in January 2006, serves as a foundation for a number of information sharing initiatives including the NSI. Available at http://www.it.ojp.gov/ default.aspx?area= globalJustice&page=1236

Privacy Impact Assessment for the eGuardian Threat Tracking System, completed in August 2008, describes the measures taken to ensure that the FBI's eGuardian system satisfies privacy requirements. Available at http://foia.fbi.gov/eguardian_threat.htm

Terrorism Information Sharing and the Nationwide Suspicious Activity Report Initiative: Background and Issues for Congress, Congressional Research Service Report (November 5, 2009), available at http://www.opencrs.com/

Appendix B - Acronyms and Abbreviations

BJA	Bureau of Justice Assistance
CICC	Criminal Intelligence Coordinating Council
CONOPS	Concept of Operations
DHS	Department of Homeland Security
DNI	Director of National Intelligence
DoD	Department of Defense
DOJ	Department of Justice
FAMS	Federal Air Marshall Service
FBI	Federal Bureau of Investigation
IACP	International Association of Chiefs of Police

IEPD	Information Exchange Package Document
ISE	Information Sharing Environment
ISE-SAR	Suspicious Activity report determined to be reasonably indicative of terrorist-related criminal activity
ITACG	Interagency Threat Assessment and Coordination Group
JTTF	Joint Terrorism Task Force
MCCA	Major Cities Chiefs Association
MCSA	Major County Sheriffs' Association
NCTC	National Counterterrorism Center
NSI	Nationwide SAR Initiative
ODNI	Office of the Director of National Intelligence
PD	Police department
PGC	Privacy Guidelines Committee
PM-ISE	Program Manager, Information Sharing Environment
SAR	Suspicious Activity Reporting

End Notes

[1] Throughout the remainder of this document, the term "NSI Privacy, Civil Rights, and Civil Liberties Framework" is normally abbreviated to "NSI Privacy Framework."

[2] See http://www.ise.gov/pages/privacy-implementing.aspx for the ISE Privacy Guidelines and related material.

[3] The ISE Privacy Guidelines and related implementation guidance can be found at http://www.ise.gov/pages/privacy-implementing.aspx.

[4] *National Strategy for Information Sharing: Successes and Challenges in Improving Terrorism-Related Information Sharing* (October 2007), pp A1-6,7 available at http://www.ise.gov/pages/documents.aspx

[5] The state or local agencies were the Boston Police Department (PD), Chicago PD, Florida Department of Law Enforcement, Houston PD, Las Vegas Metropolitan PD, Los Angeles PD, Metropolitan (Washington) DC PD, Miami-Dade Fusion Center, New York State Intelligence Center, Arizona Counter Terrorism Information Center, Seattle Police Department and the Virginia Fusion Center. FBI participated through its eGuardian system; DHS shared Federal Air Marshal Service (FAMS) data; and DoD also used eGuardian support of its Force Protection mission.

[6] See *United States v. Montero-Camargo*, 208 F.3d 1122, 1130 (9th Cir. 2000) (explaining that "sometimes conduct that may be entirely innocuous when viewed in isolation may properly be considered in arriving at a determination that reasonable suspicion exists").

[7] See *United States v. Arvizu*, 534 U.S. 273 (2002) (explaining that the reasonable suspicion determination "allows officers to draw on their own experience and specialized training to make inferences about the cumulative information available to them").

[8] Congressional Research Service Report R40901, "Terrorism Information Sharing and the Nationwide Suspicious Activity Report Initiative: Background and Issues for congress, by Mark A. Randol (November 5, 2009).

[9] *Nationwide Suspicious Activity Reporting Initiative Concept of Operations* (December 2008), pp 17-18. Available at http://www.ise.gov/pages/sar-initiative.aspx

[10] Ibid. p. 23.

[11] *ISE-SAR Functional Standard, Version 1.5* (May 2009) located at http://www.ise.gov/pages/sar-initiative.aspx

[12] NSI CONOPS., pp. 7-11.

[13] Ibid. Pp. 22-23.

[14] *Information Sharing Environment – Suspicious Activity Reporting Functional Standard and Evaluation Environment: Initial Privacy and Civil Liberties Analysis* (Sept. 2008) available at http://www.ise.gov/pages/sar-initiative.aspx

[15] *ISE-SAR Functional Standard, Version 1.5*, pp. 29-36.

[16] After a limited test to assess the value of ISE-SARs without privacy fields, it was determined that, at least for the EE, it was necessary to include privacy fields. As a result privacy policies and procedures were required to share any ISE-SARs.

[17] See http://www.prnewswire.com/news-releases/presidential-task-forcerecommendationsfor additional information.

INDEX

E

F

G

H

I

J

K

U

V

W